Mental handicap

Modern Practical Nursing Series

Mental Handicap

H. Kekstadt, R.G.N., R.N.T.

Divisional Nursing Officer
Forth Valley Health Board

D.A.A. Primrose M.D., B.L., F.R.C. Psych.,
F.R.C.P.(G), M.R.C.G.P.,

Consultant Psychiatrist and Physician Superintendent,
The Royal Scottish National Hospital, Larbert, Stirlingshire.

SECOND EDITION

WILLIAM HEINEMANN MEDICAL BOOKS LIMITED
LONDON

This book honours the memory of
the late James F. Lucas
Principal Nursing Officer
The Royal Scottish National Hospital

First published 1973 as Mental Subnormality
2nd Edition 1983
©H. Kekstadt and D.A.A. Primrose, 1983
ISBN 0-433-18279-2

Origination by Meditext, Weybridge
Printed in Great Britain by Redwood Burn Ltd, Trowbridge, Wiltshire

CONTENTS

CONTENTS—*continued*

FOREWORD

This book is intended for all those who are concerned with the day to day problems of caring for the mentally handicapped. It should help them to understand some of the reasons which cause the disabilities and provide practical suggestions for dealing with the resulting difficulties.

Although primarily addressed to nurses in training it will also be found suitable for other hospital staff such as nursing assistants, and nurses returning to work after a period away from it.

There is an increasing realisation of the need to develop community services for the handicapped and many people other than nurses are involved in this. These include social workers, child care officers, special school teachers and therapists of all kinds and we hope the book will also prove useful to them.

To the parents—the largest and most important group of all—we offer our help and support and hope that a wider understanding of mental handicap will lead to greater sympathy and help from society.

H.K.
D.A.A.P

1

Introduction

Mental handicap (mental deficiency in Scotland) is not a disease. It is a term used to cover a wide variety of conditions in which there is a lower than average intelligence. This lack of intelligence has usually been present from birth or from an early age. The term includes those people in whom something has gone wrong with development thus preventing the full growth of the intellect, as well as those who have developed normally but whose full development leaves them at the lower level of the general population. There is a similar situation with other variables such as height or weight where some people, although fully developed, may be smaller or lighter than average. Others may be smaller or lighter because of disease.

In caring for those with mental handicap one is caring for people who, for one reason or another, are unable fully to care for themselves. The inability of the individual is usually of long standing and, while he can be helped to use his limited ability to the full, he can rarely be cured.

Because of this, the qualities needed in the person who cares for the mentally handicapped are not quite the same as those required in the nurse who may be attracted to the more acute fields of nursing. Those who give such care must be:-

1 Patient, for any progress will be slow
2 Willing to persevere and keep up a high standard of care even when there is no improvement, for even the prevention of deterioration is positive gain
3 Sympathetic, for they will be dealing with people who are less able.

Thus the nurse will gain their confidence and learn to understand them. In return she will find much satisfaction and reward for her work in their very dependence, and the relationship which develops.

Although, in the foregoing, nurses have been thought of as female, there is also a need for male nurses who can act as a father figure, or elder brother, in giving continuing help and care.

This book will deal primarily with the nursing care of different kinds of mentally handicapped people in hospital. Much of it is applicable to those living at home or in hostels. In fact, most of those who are mentally handicapped do not require to go into hospital and it is usually the presence of additional disabilities that makes it advisable for about 15% of them to go into hospital, while the other 85% remain in the community.

2
History

The history of mental disorder is as old as the history of mankind. Prehistoric skulls have been found with trephine holes, possibly to let out devils. The ancient Greeks recognised brain disease and Plato distinguished between madness (mental illness) and ignorance (mental handicap). The Romans left defective children to die from exposure. Paul, writing to the Thessalonians, urged his brethren to comfort the feeble-minded. The word 'cretin' (a term for a condition in which, if untreated, there is mental subnormality) is itself derived from the word 'Christian' and in the 16th century it was realised that cretinism was associated with an enlarged thyroid gland (goitre). In 1547, the monastery of St. Mary of Bethlehem in London became a hospital for idiots and the insane and, subsequently, the word Bethlehem was contracted to 'Bedlam'.

There was little attempt to separate mental handicap from mental illness and until the end of the 18th century treatment in asylums was largely a matter of restraint. Then, in 1798, Itard in Paris tried to educate an idiot and gave some account of the psychology of mental handicap. Seguin, a pupil of Itard, founded in 1837 in Paris the first school for idiots. Pioneers in other countries were encouraged by this and in 1846 the first private school for mental defectives in England was opened at Bath, and then other institutions followed elsewhere.

As mental handicap occurs in all social classes the wealthy Victorians in Britain began to make residential provision for their own affected relatives and this provision was later extended to include the other social classes. To begin with, these places were private institutions often run as a charity and supported by voluntary subscriptions. One of the guiding principles was the provision of training so that the handicapped person became less of a public burden and, whilst the institution was providing a refuge (asylum), the inmates were expected to help with the running of it. In accordance with popular ideas at that time it was felt that a healthy body encouraged a healthy mind, and that Satan found work for idle hands to do; so physical training and work therapy were encouraged. Social training, including simple household tasks like mending and cookery, was given as well as instruction in whatever primary subjects could be learnt, such as classes in speech and telling the time and this is just as necessary today. These institutions were not intended to be hospitals in the sense of a modern general hospital but rather as therapeutic communities, and to begin with they were not intended to care for the helpless.

The Therapeutic Community is still a very valid concept for some mentally handicapped people who cannot easily fit into modern society. The more organised and regulated life becomes in cities the more difficult it becomes to participate in the normal activities of society. To try to force these people to conform to a pattern of life for which they are inadequate seems wrong when they can have more freedom and are less likely to break down in a community which is structured to their capabilities. This is an ideal which many of the Colony type of mental subnormality hospitals with large grounds try to achieve. Where there are large outdated buildings and shortages of staff the ideal may not be attained, but the system can provide care of a reasonable standard from childhood through to old age.

The Mental Deficiency Act of 1913 laid on Local Authorities the duty of providing care for certain cases of mental deficiency. This was done partly by:

1 Guardianship (p. 6)
2 Paying for accommodation in the voluntary institutions mentioned above
3 Providing new premises.

This Act also defined four classes of mental defectives according to the degree of care required and the names of three of these are still in common use.

1 *Idiot*

Someone who is unable to guard himself against common physical dangers.

2 *Imbecile*

Someone who is incapable of managing, or being taught to manage his own affairs.

3 *Feeble-minded*

Someone requiring care and supervision for his own protection or for the protection of others.

The fourth class was the moral imbecile and, like the psychopath (p. 5), these people did not need to be mentally defective.

In 1948, with the advent of the National Health Service in Great Britain, many of these institutions were nationalised and became hospitals. This has led to an emphasis on the more helpless patients and on those with more disturbed behaviour being admitted to these hospitals to the exclusion of those only requiring accommodation and simple supervision. There is once more a growing pressure on Local Authorities to provide accommodation and care in the community for those who do not require to go to hospital. Legislation to this end is embodied in the Social Services Act (1967).

In Great Britain, where the financing of the social services comes from different Government departments and Local Authorities, there is a tendency for one department to shift responsibility to another and thus the overall care of the mentally handicapped becomes fragmented. Many countries have a separate state-financed agency to provide comprehensive care for the mentally handicapped and there is much to be said for this; provided the funding is adequate.

Progress has come through the work of voluntary agencies demanding offical help and future progress will depend on these organisations acting as pressure groups on public opinion and on the politicians who in the end make the legislation.

3
Terminology

The term *mental handicap*, which has already been explained, will usually be used in this book. The International Classification of Diseases uses the term *mental retardation*, and *mental deficiency* is still used in some countries. Older terms for subgroups of the mentally handicapped were *idiot*, *imbecile* and *feeble-minded*, and *moron* was used in the United States for feeble-minded.

Mental disorder
The Mental Health Act, 1959 (S.4) introduced the general term *'mental disorder'*. Mental disorder includes:

1 Mental illness
2 Arrested or incomplete development of mind
3 Psychopathic disorder
4 Any other disorder or disability of mind.

The 1959 Act used the term 'subnormality' for arrested or incomplete development of mind. This has been changed to 'mental handicap' by the Mental Health (Amendment) Act 1982.

Severe handicap
This means a state of arrested or incomplete development of mind which includes severe impairment of intelligence and social functioning.

Mental handicap
This means a state of arrested or incomplete development of mind (not amounting to severe handicap) which includes significant impairment of intelligence and social function.

Psychopath
A psychopath is a person who has a persistent disorder or disability of mind (whether or not including subnormality of intelligence) which results in abnormally aggressive or seriously irresponsible conduct.

Mental impairment
Mental impairment and *severe mental impairment* are terms introduced by the Mental Health (Amendment) Act 1982 to replace for certain purposes the terms subnormality and severe subnormality. They are defined as states of arrested or incomplete development of mind in which there is impairment, or severe impairment, of intelligence and social

functioning together with abnormally aggressive or seriously irresponsible conduct.

Promiscuity and alcoholism
Section 4 further stated that promiscuity or other immoral conduct did not of itself imply that a person could be dealt with under the Mental Health Act and the 1982 Act repeats this with respect to alcoholism.

Medical treatment (S.147)
This includes nursing and also care and training under medical supervision.

Responsible medical officer (RMO) (S.59)
This is the medical practitioner in charge of the treatment of a patient liable to be detained in hospital for observation or treatment.

Nearest relative (S.49)
In descending order this is husband/wife; son/daughter; father/mother; brother/sister; grandparent; grandchild; uncle/aunt; nephew/niece. Where there are two or more relatives in the same group, the eldest comes first. An illegitimate child is treated as if he were the legitimate child of the mother, and a man and woman living together for more than six months can be regarded as husband and wife. If the nearest relative is absent, or disqualified from acting, then the next in line takes his place.

Guardian
A *guardian* is a person appointed by law to have custody of a person. Under the Mental Health Act guardians may be appointed to mentally handicapped persons. The regulations are similar to those in Part IV of the Act for compulsory admission to hospital (p. 138). Guardians can be paid by the Local Authority for undertaking this duty.

4
Prevalence

The prevalence of mental handicap varies from country to country and within the same country, for there is a difference between urban and rural areas. Severe handicap is usually easily recognised and the prevalence of this is fairly uniform at about 3.5 per 1000 population (it is higher at birth but many die in infancy). With simple handicap there is a large group whose intelligence is around the border-line and the deciding factor in classification is not the measured intellience level but the degree of care required. Here behaviour is all-important and as there are more stresses and difficulties encountered when living in a town than in the country the prevalence is higher in large towns. It is most accurately ascertained at about the age of 10 – 15 years, when it is over 10/1000 of the age group.

5
Development of the Child

As mental handicap is partially defined as a state of arrested or incomplete development of the mind, it is necessary in order to understand mentally handicapped people to know something of the normal development.

Development of the mind does not take place in isolation from the rest of the body and all aspects of growth require consideration.

Physical and Neurological Development

Physical development

Many people with mental handicap also have below average physical development. This slow growth may have been present before birth so that their birth weight is low. Muscular development, especially in the limbs, depends on a normal nerve supply to the limbs. Where this is damaged, as in cerebral palsy, (p. 25), then the limbs may be wasted.

Reflex actions

These are movements which take place automatically without reaching consciousness in the brain. Certain primitive reflex actions are present at birth and usually disappear by the end of the fourth month as voluntary control develops. They may persist if voluntary control does not develop. Examples are:

1 *The rooting reflex*
   When the baby's cheek touches the mother's breast, his mouth searches for the nipple.

2 *The sucking reflex*
   The baby will automatically suck when the nipple, or a similar object, is put in his mouth.

3 *The grasp reflex*
   The stroking of the palm or sole makes the fingers or toes try to close into a grip.

Milestones of development

Certain early stages of development such as sitting up, bowel control, talking, etc. are called *milestones*, and are signs of voluntary activity. When there is mental handicap there is usually delay in reaching most of these milestones. Some average ages for the normal baby are:

Lift head from pillow—4 months
Sit unaided—7 months
Walk a few steps—18 months
Speech, single words—12 months
Speech, short sentences—2 years
Bowel control—18 months
Bladder control—2 years.

It must be emphasised that these ages are averages only and there is considerable variation within the normal range.

Social and Intellectual Development

At the same time as these physical controls are being developed the baby is becoming aware of other people and of his place amongst them.

Elementary socialisation

There is a first *elementary period of socialisation* which lasts for about 18 months. At age one week crying may be meaningful, smiling is present by 6 weeks and at 4 – 5 months there is selective attention to faces. By 8 months a normal baby has sufficient idea of his own position relative to his surroundings to move about purposefully, and at one year he can obey simple commands and refrain from forbidden acts.

Domestic socialisation

The next stage is *domestic socialisation* and lasts from about 1½ years to 4 – 5 years of age. Here the child is learning to adapt to the environment and

to develop interpersonal relationships. In doing so he must develop personal habits which are suitable for communal living. By the age of 2 or 3 years the child is aware of his own separate existence and there is often a period of wilful resistance to adult direction and training. Despite this rejection he still considers himself part of the family unit.

Communal socialisation
After the domestic socialisation there is a third stage of *communal socialisation* when the child participates in organised play and goes to school. He learns to be less dependent on the family and later, in adolescence, identifies himself with his own age group and tends to rebel against adult and established society.

Piaget's Theories

The Swiss psychologist, Piaget, whilst recognising physical growth and the development of the nervous and hormonal systems, looked especially at the development of mental growth and behaviour patterns.

Sensorimotor stage
Piaget's first stage up to age 18 months dealt with the development of sensations going to the brain and with movement—'sensorimotor'. At the end of this stage the child should be able to appreciate objects which he can touch and handle.

Symbolic thought

The second stage is the development of *symbolic thought*. Here the memory of objects develops and the child realises when something is absent and will search for a lost toy. He learns that an object is the same size whether near or far away and that it is the same shape whether looked at from the front or the side. Imagination develops in thought and language and in play with 'let's pretend' games. Since thought is no longer restricted as in the sensorimotor stage by what is actually present this allows for an enormous expansion of mental images and of language.

Understanding relationships

The child having learnt, firstly by the age of 18 months his own relationship to other objects so that he can move about from one place to another and back again and, secondly by the age of 4 years (in the second stage) to remember things in their absence, has then to go through a stage of understanding objects and people in relation to each other and of them to himself. This interpretative stage takes up to the age of 7 years.

From the age of 7 until the age of about 11 years there is a stage where thoughts about objects are grouped and classified and the concept of numbers and things in order is developed (concrete operational thinking). This leads on to a pre-adolescent stage of ideas and ideals where there is interest in the abstract and in considering the future.

Sexual Development

The understanding of the mind in sexual development is largely based on the work of Sigmund Freud.

In the infant early pleasurable sensations are centred on the mouth and on feeding. This is the oral stage which lasts until the baby is aged about 18 months. It is succeeded by an anal phase in which the production of a bowel motion produces pleasure and paying attention to this may assist in toilet training. This phase continues until about 3 years of age when it is followed by a genital stage where pleasure is obtained by touching the external genitalia and then there is sometimes an infantile form of masturbation which is quite harmless.

These stages are followed in early childhood by a period of sexual curiosity and sometimes exhibitionism and then there is a quiet period from about seven years of age until adolescence.

More recently, following studies on the imprinting process in baby animals and birds, some people have thought that a similar process may occur with human infants when an attachment to an external object, such as a doll or cuddly toy, is formed. This attachment helps to reinforce the inborn sexual instincts and when maturity develops it influences the sights which, particularly in men, arouse sexual desire. Abnormalities in this imprinting may lead to homosexual, rather than heterosexual desires.

Adolescence

This is the stage of change from child to adult and lasts for several years. During it there is a growth spurt with increase in height, muscular development, and the appearance of the secondary sexual characteristics. In the male there is deepening of the voice, growth of hair on face, axillae and pubis and the enlargement of the genitalia. In the female the breasts develop and there is growth of axillary and pubic hair; there is enlargement of the genitalia and menstruation commences.

Adolescents like to associate with their own age group. During adolescence sexual desire develops and initially these feelings are often homosexual and particularly in the male, may result in homosexual activities.

With increasing maturity there is a change to heterosexuality and many friendships with the opposite sex develop. The male becomes more aggressive and the female more subject to wide variations of mood. Emotions are felt acutely and there are often high ideals and ethical standards; mental capacity reaches its peak, and hope and ambition become driving forces. All this may lead to questioning and rejection of much of the older adult pattern of life and a demand for independence. The rejection and questioning can result in feelings of insecurity, and the desire for independence to experimentation in order to gain experience. In some adolescents this leads to drug taking and delinquent behaviour.

In those who are mentally handicapped development is slow and may be arrested at any of these stages. The realisation of this helps in the understanding of behaviour which may be much behind the physical development, and the need for tolerance of this has to be appreciated.

6

Intelligence Tests

Before someone can be regarded as having below average intelligence there must be agreement on what is the normal range of intelligence for people of that age and so standard tests are required. These tests consist of different tasks which test various aspects of intellectual performance. The person must first have the capacity to understand the task and then the ability and willingness to perform it. The validity of the tests may be impaired if the subject is tired, or depressed, or taking sedative drugs, or not cooperating. The tasks may be:

1 Verbal—with question and answer
2 Visual—where pictures or designs are shown.

Performance may require a movement such as building bricks or threading beads, or copying designs.

Memory and coordination are important and the tasks are graded with each one more difficult than the preceding. The tests are devised so that the effects of previous schooling and cultural background are minimised thus ensuring that once the tests have been standardised they can have widespread application. There are many different intelligence tests and some of these have been adapted and standardised for different countries and cultures.

Vineland Social Maturity Scale
An early test was the *Vineland Social Maturity Scale* which measured the attainments of a child in social terms, such as whether he can laugh, sit up, walk, feed, is toilet trained, plays with other children, etc. Marks are given for each accomplishment and then added up to give a total which can be expressed as an Equivalent Social Age and, when compared with the true age of the child, can be expressed as a Social Quotient (SQ), For example a social age of 1.5 years in a child whose real age is 6 years would have an SQ of $1.5/6 \times 100 = 25$.

Wechsler Intelligence Tests
The Wechsler Intelligence Tests are for children (WISC) and Adults (WAIS). These tests are less suitable for those with very low intelligence. In these tests there are two main divisions, one measuring verbal ability, the other measuring performance.

Each division has five subgroups with an extra alternative for children.

The verbal subgroups are:

1 *Information*
   Questions of increasing difficulty are asked to test general knowledge, e.g. How many days in a week?

2 *Comprehension*
   Designed to test common sense understanding, e.g Why is it better to build a house of bricks than of wood?

3 *Arithmetic*
   Simple problems are asked, e.g. James had 8 marbles and he bought 6 more. How many marbles did he have altogether?

4 *Similarities*
   This tests understanding of where things are alike, e.g. In what way are a plum and a peach alike?

5 *Vocabulary or memory test*
   The final test is either a vocabulary test or a memory test in which numbers are given and then have to be repeated in the correct order (*Digit Span*).

The performance subgroups are:

1 *Picture completion*
   Picture of objects with parts missing—the missing part to be pointed out.

2 *Picture arrangement*
Pictures to be arranged in order to tell a story.

3 *Block design*
Coloured bricks have to be arranged to match a pattern.

4 *Object assembly*
The picture of an object is cut up into pieces and has to be reassembled to make the picture.

5 *Digit symbol or coding*
Copying down of signs according to an example.

In some of these tests speed is important and there is a time limit with bonus marks for quick performance.

Terman-Merrill/Stanford-Binet test
An older and well standardised test is the Terman-Merrill modification of the Stanford-Binet Scale which was originally designed in 1907. This test is more related to scholastic ability and the sub-tests are not separated into verbal and performance groups as in the Wechsler tests. The final result gives the mental age of the child and, by relating this to the actual age of the child, the Intelligence Quotient is found.

Intelligence Quotient
The *Intelligence Quotient* (IQ) is a number which is arrived at after a series of tests has been carried out on a person. The tests are marked so that a person of average intelligence would score 100, those above average score more and those below average score less. A person's performance at different times is not constant and there is some variation between different tests. The average person will score between 85 and 115. The IQ is calculated thus: $IQ = MA/CA \times 100$. It is written as a number and not as a percentage, e.g. IQ of a 12 year old child with a mental age of 9 years is $9/12 \times 100 = 75$.

An IQ of less than 70 is taken to indicate mental handicap and below 50 severe handicap. In mental handicap the performance is poor over a wide range of sub-tests and if a very wide range of ability is found in the sub-tests then there may be a physical or psychological cause depressing the score in some of the tests and this must be looked for, e.g. a child with poor vision may have good verbal scores and poor performance ones. The IQ is not the only factor to be considered and where there is any doubt further examinations by doctor and psychologist should be carried out.

Personality tests
Personality can be taken to mean the sum total of the way in which a person

usually reacts to changes in his environmental situations. It assumes that a person will react more or less in the same way in similar situations so that there is a certain consistency in the behaviour pattern.

Personality tests have been designed to measure this in terms of the dominant emotions and drives of the person. None of the tests has so far been standardised for the mentally handicapped, and the observations of an intelligent parent or nurse over a period of time should give a more reliable indication of the personality than any of the present tests.

Progress Assessment Charts
In order to help to assess the progress of a child and to highlight any specific defects, periodic assessments should be made and convenient charts for recording the state of development have been produced. One of the most useful is the Progress Assessment Chart (Gunzburg)—see diagram below— in which developmental attainments are shown in a circle and each quadrant deals with a specific area:

1 Communication
2 Socialisation
3 Occupation
4 Self-help

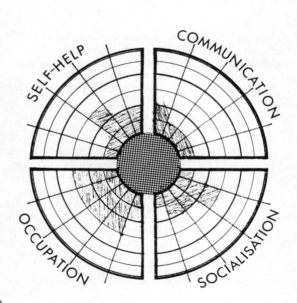

These are useful records but are no substitute for the daily observation and encouragement which a nurse should be giving to all her patients. When there is good care the nurse will be aware of any progress, and also of any lack of attainment which requires extra training without waiting for the completion of charts to initiate action.

7

Causes and Clinical Conditions

The causes of mental handicap are in many cases unknown but there are certain abnormalities known to be associated with mental handicap and some of these are discussed.

Chromosomal Conditions

One large group is that in which there is abnormality in the chromosome pattern of the individual.

Chromosomes are the structures in the nucleus of a cell which carry the genetic material which is transmitted from one generation to the next. The fertilised human egg cell normally has 23 pairs of chromosomes, one of each pair having come from each parent. One of these pairs determines the sex of the individual. Of this pair, one will be an X chromosome and will have come from the mother, the other sex chromosome comes from the father and may be an X or a Y. If it is an X the child will be a female with two X sex chromosomes, if a Y then a male with XY sex chromosomes. The other 22 pairs are called *autosomes*.

The chromosomes can be seen under a microscope. They are of different sizes and are grouped according to size from the largest to the smallest and the autosomes are numbered from 1 to 22. Sometimes there is difficulty in distinguishing one from another and so they are also grouped:

Group A	Nos. 1, 2, 3	
Group B	Nos. 4, 5	
Group C	Nos. 6, 7, 8, 9, 10, 11, 12	X
Group D	Nos. 13, 14, 15	
Group E	Nos. 16, 17, 18	
Group F	Nos. 19, 20	
Group G	Nos. 21, 22	Y

The X chromosome is included in the C group and the Y in the G group. The sex chromosomes can be seen under the microscope in cells from the mucous membrane of the mouth using special stains and illumination. The other chromosomes are usually obtained from white cells from blood, or cells from skin. With special staining, bands can be seen across the chromosomes and the positions of these bands help in identifying a chromosome. Chromosome abnormalities may arise when:

1 There are one or more chromosomes too many
2 One is absent

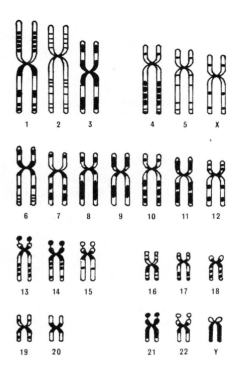

3   Part of a chromosome is missing
4   Shape of a chromosome is distorted.

Translocation

Translocation is the term used when during the division of the germ cell one chromosome (usually small) joins on to another one. Most commonly this occurs in Down's syndrome between a No. 21 and a No. 15 chromosome. The joined chromosome looks like a large one and the total chromosome number is 46 instead of 47.

There is translocation in about 2 per cent of mothers of Down's syndrome children so that their total chromosome number is 45. Clinically they are normal but during the production of an ovum there is a 1:4 chance of the No. 21 chromosome which was translocated appearing as an extra chromosome, and if fertilised resulting in trisomy 21.

Translocation can be diagnosed from the chromosomes in the white blood cells, and when a person is known to have translocation then any pregnancy can be tested for trisomy by using amniotic fluid obtained during the 3rd to 4th month of pregnancy. There is then the possibility of therapeutic termination.

Mosaicism
This term is used when some of the cells of the body have one chromosome constitution and other cells of the body have a different chromosome constitution.

Down's syndrome (Mongolism)

Down's syndrome (DS), or mongolism, is the commonest abnormality affecting the autosomes and is associated with an extra chromosome, No. 21 in the G group, or *trisomy 21*. This condition occurs in about 1 in 700 births but is more common when the mother is older. The effects of the extra chromosome in mongolism are added on to the rest of the genetic material in the fertilised egg and so, although there are characteristic similarities in mongols, there are also wide variations within the condition. In intelligence they may have an IQ of over 50 or under 20, but most fall within the range of 20 – 50. Because the whole development is affected other defects may occur and at birth half of all mongols have congenital heart disease and many of these die young.

Appearance in Down's syndrome
The characteristic which gave rise to the name *mongolism* (first described by Langdon Down in 1866) is the fact that the line between the eyelids slants down and in towards the nose and there are folds of skin at the inner angle of the eye. In addition to these, such persons are usually small in stature and have small rounded heads and a large coarse tongue. The hair is usually sparse and straight and the skin is coarse and dry. The hands tend to be broad and clumsy and the palm itself sometimes has a single transverse crease. The fingers are short and the little finger may curve inwards.

In the eye a squint is a common finding. Conjunctivitis frequently occurs and cataracts may be present. There is also an increased frequency of upper respiratory infection. Sexual development is retarded, but females may menstruate and can become pregnant.

X-ray of the chest may show one rib missing.

The life span in Down's syndrome is less than average but of those who survive to 5 years of age most live to 40 years of age, after which the death rate rises rapidly.

Most persons with Down's syndrome are good natured and have a sense of rhythm; they may be good mimics and give the appearance of being more intelligent than they really are. Many can be looked after at home until old age and those who come into hospital are more likely to have congenital heart disease, or be blind, or be so backward that they remain incontinent and do not learn to feed themselves.

The incidence of epilepsy in Down's syndrome is about the same as in the general population, but the seizures are usually less frequent and less severe. Epileptic seizures occurring for the first time in older Down's syndrome people usually indicate serious mental deterioration.

Sex chromosome abnormalities
In females it sometimes happens that there is only one X sex chromosome (total number 45) and a condition also occurs in which there are more than two X sex chromosomes.

Turner's syndrome
Is the condition with only one X chromosome.

These women are often of normal intellience. They are small and usually have webbing of the neck. There is poor sexual development with amenorrhoea and sterility.

Extra X sex chromosomes
Where there are extra X sex chromosomes there is usually a degree of mental handicap. Sexual development may be normal in females with XXX, but about half of XXXX females are sterile.

Klinefelter's syndrome
A male with no X chromosomes does not occur, but males are found with more than one X chromosome (*Klinefelter's syndrome*). They are usually mentally handicapped and are effeminate with poorly developed sex organs. This condition sometimes occurs in Down's syndrome. The greater the number of extra X chromosomes the more abnormal the person.

Males with more than one Y chromosome tend to be tall and may be aggressive. They may be of normal intelligence or mildly handicapped.

Abnormal X chromosome
Abnormalities of the X chromosome are being discovered with increasing

frequency amongst mentally handicapped males. The abnormal chromosome may be inherited from an otherwise normal mother, and female children may carry the defective chromosome, although seldom themselves showing any other defect. In the affected adult male the testes may be abnormally enlarged, and the ears may be large, flat and prominent.

Genetic Conditions

The individual factors of inheritance which are carried on the chromosomes are called *genes* and each chromosome in a pair (except for the X and Y) has a similar complement of genes. Thus one gene of each pair has come from the father and the other from the mother. Sometimes both genes of a pair are necessary to produce an effect and then the genes are called *recessive*; sometimes only one is necessary and then the gene producing the effect is called *dominant*. Where several genes are involved then the term *multifactorial* is used.

During inheritance a gene may undergo a change and such a change is called a *mutation*. Most mutations are lethal but some survive to produce a change in the developing embryo. X-rays and other forms of radiation can cause mutations and genetic damage.

Epiloia, or *tuberose sclerosis* is a condition in which mental handicap is associated with epilepsy and skin abnormalities. At birth there may be oval leaf-shaped areas in the skin in which pigment is lacking, but the characteristic rash and nodules of *adenoma sebaceum* which develop across the nose and cheeks may not appear until later in childhood, or adolescence. Fibrous nodules occur in the brain and sometimes in other internal organs. Some cases arise as the result of mutations, but in the others it is inherited from one or other parent. Half the children from an affected parent are likely to be affected but as the severity of the condition is so variable it is sometimes so mild as to escape diagnosis. The skin rash and nodules may not be present at birth and may not appear until the child is aged 3 years or more.

A recessive genetic condition which may cause mental handicap is phenylketonuria (PKU). This is a biochemical upset in which an enzyme which helps to digest phenylalanine is absent. Phenylalanine is one of the amino-acids present in protein and unless it can be properly digested it poisons the developing nervous system. A drop of blood taken about one week after birth from every baby born in the U.K. is tested for this condition by the Guthrie test. If the test is positive follow up tests are required to confirm the diagnosis. When the condition is diagnosed it is important to reduce severely the amount of phenylalanine in the food. Special milk and food preparations are available for this and the diet should be continued for several years until the nervous system has developed. Thereafter a more normal diet can be tried.

Affected children are fairer than they would otherwise be as the condition reduces the production of body pigment. When untreated in addition to mental retardation there is often hyperactive behaviour and a tendency to eczema and skin rashes.

Should an affected woman plan to have a baby, or become pregnant, she should immediately go back on to the special diet so as not to affect the unborn child.

Other Conditions

Cretinism
This is a condition in which there is mental handicap and retardation of growth. It is caused by insufficient thyroid hormone, and as iodine is necessary to make the hormone, it used to be common in mountainous regions where the drinking water was lacking in iodine.

In most countries iodine is now added to the salt and the condition is uncommon, but it can result from other causes. As with phenylketonuria a drop of blood taken from the baby shortly after birth can be tested for lack of thyroid hormone and when this is diagnosed synthetic hormone can be taken by mouth, and the baby then develops normally.

Cerebral anoxia
This is lack of sufficient oxygen to the brain. It may occur during pregnancy where, for example, the placental blood supply is inadequate, or during prolonged labour, or it may occur shortly after birth if the baby is slow to breathe. It is one of the causes of cerebral palsy.

Cerebral palsy
This is a condition in which there is paralysis of the limbs as a result of brain damage prior to, or around the time of birth. It is not a single disease, and has several different causes, one of the commonest being insufficient oxygen to the brain (see above). In about half of the cases there is also mental handicap. All four limbs may be affected (quadriplegia) or both upper or lower limbs (diplegia). Where one side of the body is affected it is called hemiplegia. Hemiplegia is often due to more localised brain damage and then the general level of intelligence is less affected.

The paralysis may present as a limpness of the limbs (flaccid type) or as stiffness (spastic type). There is also an athetoid type which is characterised by waving and jerkiness of the affected limbs when movement is attempted.

Microcephaly

The head is much smaller than normal in this condition and most of the reduction in size is above the level of the eyes and ears. The scalp may be too big for the underlying skull and have loose transverse folds in it. The skull itself is usually long and narrow. Stature is small. There is usually severe handicap, and sometimes cerebral palsy as well. It is sometimes sex-linked and is thus more common in males.

Hydrocephalus

This term is used when the head is distended as a result of too much cerebrospinal fluid in the brain. There are several different causes and if it is present at birth the intelligence is more likely to be affected than in those cases where the hydrocephalus develops later, such as following meningitis. Operations are performed to put a tube with a one-way valve into the brain to drain the excess fluid into the large veins of the neck or into the abdomen. When successful this prevents the enlargement of the head, and may prevent further deterioration of the intelligence.

Spina bifida

This is a condition in which the development of the spinal cord and its coverings is incomplete. All degrees of defect occur and shortly after birth it may be necessary to perform an operation to cover the incomplete part. Hydrocephalus is sometimes present together with spina bifida and operations for both conditions may be required.

Spina bifida may be diagnosed antenatally by testing blood taken from the mother between the 16th and 18th week of pregnancy for α-feto-protein. When the result is abnormal the fetus can be examined by using an ultrasonic scanner and any severe cases will be shown up. Therapeutic termination is then a possibility.

Infection

Certain infections in the mother during pregnancy may affect the unborn child and sometimes these interfere with the development of the brain. For instance, German measles (rubella) contracted in the first three months of pregnancy may result in blindness, deafness, or mental retardation. Other infections, such as syphilis or toxoplasmosis, may also cause brain damage.

Brain infections (encephalitis and meningitis) contracted in early childhood may cause widespread damage, with resulting mental handicap; examples are herpes simplex virus encephalitis and tuberculous meningitis.

Rhesus factor incompatibility

When a mother has a rhesus-negative blood group she may develop antibodies to the rhesus factor if she becomes pregnant with a rhesus-positive baby. These antibodies can cross the placenta and in a subsequent pregnancy they may cause brain damage to the developing child with resulting mental handicap, and cerebral palsy. This condition can be tested for and, if present, the baby can be treated at birth (or shortly before) with blood transfusions. Rhesus-negative mothers can be given injections of antibodies immediately after each delivery (or miscarriage) to neutralise antigens from a rhesus-positive baby.

Injury and haemorrhage
Direct injury during pregnancy, at birth, or afterwards, rarely causes damage to the brain widespread enough to affect the overall level of intelligence without affecting life itself. However, widespread bleeding into the brain can cause mental handicap and this may be from multiple small haemorrhages as in purpura, or from repeated limited bleeding, as in haemophilia.

Other conditions
There are many other conditions associated with mental handicap but they are uncommon and may be found in some of the books mentioned at the end of this book for further reading.

Mental handicap due to physical defects
A mentally handicapped person may not develop in relation to his environment because of sensory defects such as blindness or deafness, or because of a motor defect such as in cerebral palsy when he cannot move his body or limbs to familiarise himself with objects. Between the input of stimuli to the brain and the resultant action of the body which is dependent on nerves coming from the brain, there is the connecting mechanism in the brain. Where this is damaged an appropriate or controlled response may not be obtained. For example, a hyperkinetic (overactive) child may hear and see and be able to move all his limbs, but his actions are not sensible. He may do things *to* objects (or people) but not *with* them; again 'autistic' children can hear and see (perhaps abnormally) but there seems to be a defect in the internal brain mechanism which prevents them from translating the sensory input into useful speech or action.

When a satisfactory response to stimulation cannot be given by the child interest in him by his parents and others tends to diminish and then less stimulation is given and a vicious circle develops. When the defect is present from birth the mental condition may appear to deteriorate as the rest of the body develops and the defect becomes more obvious.

A person of normal intelligence who has brain damage tries to compensate for the defect by training his other faculties to a greater degree. For example, a blind man develops a more acute sense of hearing, and the earlier this is begun the better the results. Where the intelligence is also impaired it is all the more necessary to concentrate on early stimulation of the senses and to continue it for a prolonged period even when the response seems to be very slow, so that the maximum development can be obtained. There is, however, no good evidence to show that continuous stimulation is any better than more moderate periodic stimulation.

Social deprivation
Where a child is deprived of the normal stimuli to development, as when he is isolated and not given attention, then mental development is retarded. Such children usually progress spectacularly when placed in a more stimulating and emotionally satisfying environment, and sometimes the mere removal from a bad environment is sufficient to produce improvement.

Mental Illness

Mental illnesses can occur in the mentally handicapped but the way in which they present is affected by the stage of development of the patient. Like young children the handicapped have not attained a mature personality and so their response to mental stress is more primitive. Mental illnesses can be thought of as abnormal reactions to stresses which may be internal or external or both.

It is customary to divide mental illnesses into:

1 *The neuroses*
   In these the patient is able to realise his own condition (i.e. has insight), and that he is mentally upset.

2 *The psychoses*
   In these insight is impaired and there may be delusions.

However, the boundary between the one and the other is often blurred and patients may have symptoms of both and the symptoms can change during the course of an illness.

Some of the mental illnesses which afflict the handicapped are akin to the neuroses and can best be described in terms of the *adjustment disorders of childhood*, e.g:

1 *Habit disorders*
   Such as head banging or rocking, and other repetitive movements.

2 *Behaviour disorders*

Such as temper tantrums, dishonesty, destructiveness and cruelty. Sometimes the loss of emotional control may resemble the attacks of hysteria seen in persons of normal intelligence but immature personality.

There are other patients who show enough of the characteristics of the more serious psychoses to be so diagnosed. Such psychoses are:

Schizophrenia

In this condition the patient is unable to think clearly. Thoughts may be confused and there is a loss of touch with reality. There are *delusions* which although not founded on fact are none the less real to the patient, and he may believe that someone is persecuting him, or that he is the reincarnation of an important person. These symptoms may vary in intensity during the illness.

Sometimes there are *hallucinations* when the patient hears, sees, smells or feels things which are not actually present. Auditory hallucinations are the commonest and then the patient may be seen adopting a listening attitude or carrying on a conversation with an imaginary person.

Often there is a lack of willpower and the schizophrenic adopts a withdrawn and negative attitude. If he adopts a motionless trance-like state, this is called *catatonia*, and usually there is a minimal reaction to stimuli such as questions or movement. Occasionally a catatonic patient can become excited and aggressive.

Throughout a schizophrenic illness there is an overall lack of emotional response which is called *bluntening of affect*. Sometimes an emotional response is inappropriate or incongruous.

In treating schizophrenia it is important for the nurse to try to establish an emotional relationship with the patient to counteract the loss of affect, and to try to keep him in touch with reality. She can help by encouraging simple activities in the ward, or occupational therapy department and by forcing the patient to use some part of his mind. Drugs of the phenothiazine groups, such as chlorpromazine are very useful in treating schizophrenia. Some of these are long-acting and may be given by injection, and are especially useful for treating out-patients.

Autism

This is a term which is rather loosely used to describe children who are withdrawn and do not develop a normal relationship with other people. This lack of emotional response is usually present from infancy and typically the baby is not cuddly and does not give a smile of recognition. There is often an abnormal attraction to shiny objects, and a strong objection to changes in routine. A normal use of language fails to develop. Many autistic children are also mentally handicapped, but in these the development of milestones such as crawling, sitting, feeding, bowel control, etc. is not so retarded as the mental state. Treatment of these patients depends on the establishment of an emotional relationship and this requires prolonged and sympathetic handling of the child by those caring for him. Sometimes music is helpful in developing contact with the child.

Mania
This is a kind of psychosis in which the mind is grossly overactive and the mood is abnormally elevated. It is unreal and stimulating, but lacks sustained direction, and speech and actions jump from one topic to another. There may be delusions of grandeur, power or wealth. These may be spoken of so convincingly that there is at first a tendency to believe them. The patient may continue to be so overactive that he exhausts himself and much kindness, tact, and firmness are required in nursing him. Drugs are often helpful and ECT (electro-convulsive therapy) may be useful in high-grade patients.

Hypomania
This is a lesser degree of mania.

Depressive psychosis
This is a state in which the mood is miserable or utterly desperate and for which no specific cause can be found. It may be of long duration and tends to recur and in some patients may alternate with mania. Anti-depressive drugs are often necessary in these patients and sometimes ECT is used in high-grade patients.

Suicide
Mentally handicapped people do not often commit suicide but any suggestion by a patient that he will do so, or any actual attempt, must be taken seriously and the doctor informed. At the least it is an indication that the person is upset and the reasons for this should be sought. A mentally handicapped person may attach great importance to actions or objects which seem relatively trivial to others, and the reasons given for contemplating or attempting suicide should have proper attention paid to them even though they seem insignificant.

8

Epilepsy in the Mentally Handicapped

Epilepsy is not in itself a disease but an indication of a temporary disturbance in the working of the brain.

Most people with epilepsy are of normal intellience. In the mentally handicapped epilepsy is relatively common and in particular amongst those in hospital where up to one third of the patients may be subject to seizures (or fits). It is one of the factors which leads to institutional care and which makes discharge and employment more difficult.

Epileptic attacks are usually divided into two groups, *grand mal* (major) and *petit mal* (minor) and both may occur in the same person. In grand mal epilepsy the person loses consciousness and may fall to the ground and empty the bladder or bowel. In petit mal epilepsy the loss of consciousness is so transient that the person looks pale and dazed but can usually continue his previous occupation after a momentary pause and without falling to the ground. The distinction is important as the drug treatment of grand mal may be different from petit mal.

The pattern of a typical grand mal seizure is:

1 *Aura*

An 'aura' in which the patient may give a cry or have a peculiar sensation of taste or smell or seem to hear a noise, and he may then fall to the ground. The aura may be momentary and may not be remembered.

2 *Tonic phase*

The next stage is one of rigidity when the patient lies with muscles contracted.

3 *Clonic phase*

This is followed after some seconds by convulsions when the muscles relax and contract and the whole body shakes.

4 *Drowsiness*

When the clonic phase wears off there is a period of drowsiness which may last for a minute or two, or for some hours.

5 *Post-epileptic automatism*

This occasionally occurs after a seizure. The patient is physically active but the brain is still confused. This can occasionally result in violence to others or to the patient himself.

Sometimes a succession of fits occurs and this is called *status epilepticus*. It requires urgent treatment as it can be fatal.

Epilepsy is, in some persons, more common at night than during the day and a seizure may not be observed when the patient is asleep, and a wet bed or prolonged drowsiness in the morning may be signs of this.

A febrile illness may precipitate a seizure and, in some women seizures are more common about the time of menstruation. The flicker from a television screen can start a seizure and epileptic patients should not be allowed to sit close to a television set.

Infantile seizures (Salaam attacks). This is a form of epilepsy, beginning in the first year of life, in which there are sudden brief repetitive contraction spasms of the limbs and body. They are often associated with mental handicap and a particular abnormality in the EEG.

Temporal lobe epilepsy. This is a form of epilepsy due to damage in one of the temporal lobes of the brain.

Electroencephalogram (EEG)
An electroencephalogram is a tracing of the electrical activity of the brain. In epilepsy a particular kind of wave pattern may be present such as in petit mal or it may demonstrate damage in one area of the brain, such as in temporal lobe epilepsy. The EEG can show an epileptic tracing although no seizures have occurred and this means that the tendency is there. Even when seizures have occurred the characteristic tracings may not be obtained. Drugs affect the tracings and so if a patient is going to have an EEG it is essential to know what drugs he is having.

Treatment of a seizure
The immediate aim is to prevent the patient from injuring himself especially in falling. Patients who have frequent seizures may wear padded helmets to protect their heads and sit in special epileptic chairs with a back which slants backwards, so that when a seizure occurs they are more likely to fall back in the chair than on to the floor. Once the seizure has started, care should be taken that the involuntary convulsive movements do not result in injury. If the jaw is convulsing, some object, e.g. a padded spoon, should be placed in the mouth to prevent the tongue being bitten, and the head turned to one side. False teeth should be removed and are better not used by epileptics who have frequent attacks. After the convulsive stage has passed the patient should be put to bed if drowsy, and kept under observation in case, either further attacks develop, or the patient exhibits disturbed behaviour before becoming fully conscious.

Drugs

Most people with epilepsy take drugs routinely to prevent the onset of seizures. There are many different drugs and any one person may require to take more than one of these drugs two or three times daily. In status epilepticus drugs may have to be given by injection, and in addition to those which are used for the prevention of seizures, intravenous diazepam may be useful, especially in children.

Epileptic personality

Some patients with epilepsy have periodic disorders of mood when they become aggressive and irritable. This may be followed by a seizure and thereafter their mood improves until the next time. Treatment may reduce the frequency of seizures but the upsets of mood can still occur and stronger sedation may be required until the mood changes. The nurse can help greatly if she recognises and reports these changes of mood.

Epileptic equivalents

These are periodic violent outbursts which take the place of an epileptic seizure.

Hysteria

Hysterical fits occur amongst high-grade mentally handicapped females and some of these imitate epilepsy fairly well, but in these fits patients do not usually hurt themselves in falling, nor become incontinent of urine, and following a hysterical attack there is seldom drowsiness. These points along with her knowledge of the individual patient will help the nurse to distinguish hysteria from true epilepsy.

9
Behaviour Disorders

There are often kinds of behaviour which cause little concern in very young children who will be expected to grow out of them. Examples are head-banging or a child biting itself, throwing objects about or destroying them, playing with or eating faeces, and uncontrolled emotion expressed by screaming or aggression. When such behaviour persists into later childhood and beyond it may be dangerous to the person, or to others, and this is one of the commonest reasons for requiring admission to hospital.

There is sometimes an underlying physical reason, such as when a blind child pokes its eyes, or a deaf child bangs its ears to cause sensory stimulation which is otherwise lacking. Medical reasons for behaviour disturbance include an abnormal blood sugar, and a raised uric acid level in the blood, and sometimes undesirable sexual behaviour may be due to abnormal imprinting in infancy (see Sexual Development p. 13). Boredom and lack of attention may be a cause and if this results in getting the desired attention then the behaviour may become an established pattern, even when the attention results in forceful disapproval.

Treatment will depend on the cause and so a thorough examination should be made, including a careful enquiry into the early background of the person, as well as any medical or psychological tests which may be indicated. Drugs may be helpful where a specific abnormality is found. Where there is epilepsy or other underlying brain damage drugs can be of great benefit in helping emotional control, and where there is associated mental illness with thought disorder or depression the drugs normally used to treat these conditions are equally helpful in the mentally handicapped.

In studying the unwanted behaviour questions to be asked include: How often and when does it occur? Is it related to meal times, or the presence or absence of a particular person? And what events result in its termination? Once the answers to these and similar questions are known then an individual plan of treatment can be drawn up. Treatment should concentrate on encouraging alternative acceptable behaviour rather than drawing further attention to the undesired behaviour. Prolonged treatment is usually required and is not always successful, and when not, caring in a controlled environment may be the best way to minimise further injury and damage.

The essence of nursing care for patients with behaviour disorders is good management, and this includes the adaptation of the environment to accommodate such behaviour as may be considered reasonable and also to control it when it becomes too disturbing. Such management requires an understanding of the individual patient which cannot be taught in the classroom, but can only be acquired by practical experience and in-service training. It is essential to be able to divide the patients into compatible groups and desirable to have more than one group to suit each class of patient so that where there is a conflict within a group, there is an alternative group to which one or more of the patients may go.

The nurse, from working with her patients, will learn to know what antagonisms exist between patients, or patients and staff, and also when too strong an emotional attachment is developing. In this way she should be able to anticipate trouble before it arises and take appropriate action. This may involve keeping a patient in bed, or in the villa, rather than allowing him to go to his occupation; it may mean arranging for a change of occupation or the separation of two patients who are too emotionally involved. If the villas are staffed at different levels according to the needs of the patients, then when necessary a patient who becomes more disturbed can be moved into a villa with a higher staffing ratio until his behaviour settles down again.

A scheme of incentives should be developed in which improving behaviour results in more attractive occupations, more recreational opportunities and greater freedom, whilst disruptive behaviour results in the opposite. Any such system must of course be simple enough to be understood by the patients and must be seen by the patients as a whole to work fairly so that the promotion, or otherwise, of one patient is an example and encouragement to the rest.

Much of the antisocial behaviour which necessitates the admission of a patient is a reaction to an environment with which he cannot cope and the more urban and organised society becomes the more difficult it is for a handicapped person to fit in. In hospital the more homely the atmosphere the better, but with patients who have been admitted because of a pattern of disturbed behaviour, this must be balanced against the need for observation. Space is a very important factor in reducing tensions and where the patients have adequate dayroom space and freedom to wander in the grounds then behaviour patterns improve very much. Common dangers have of course to be guarded against as many cannot appreciate the full consequences of their actions, e.g. shrubs in the grounds should not have poisonous berries, and machinery in workshops may need extra safety guards. Fire is fascinating for some patients so matches and cigarette lighters must be under strict control.

Violent patients
When a patient is admitted to hospital because of aggressive outbursts

then, as stated above, the removal from his familiar background in which there are stresses to which he may be reacting, is often enough to produce improvement and diminish the frequency of the outbursts. If there is plenty of space in the hospital and its grounds then this reduces the likelihood of conflict arising between the aggressive patient and others. It is important not to overload the nursing staff and to ensure that patients are cared for in wards where the facilities and staff are adequate for the violent episodes which may occur from time to time. The potentially violent patient requires a lot of observation so that any disturbing factors can be removed as soon as possible. The nurse may come to recognise, by observing changes in the usual pattern of behaviour, that a patient is becoming upset. By taking appropriate action, such as putting him to bed, or talking to him in a quiet room she may prevent an aggressive outburst. Sometimes disturbed behaviour is a reaction to a promise made by relatives and not kept, or because of an anniversary which has been ignored. A letter to the relative by the nurse or doctor may produce a response which quietens the patient's anxieties.

The violent episode
On occasions sedative drugs, physical restraint and isolation become necessary to prevent a patient damaging himself, other patients, or staff and property. Physical control should be firm but not violent or punitive and only the minimum amount of force should be used. If other staff are near their assistance should be sought for three or four people may be required to restrain one patient, and the more people there are the less injury there is likely to be. When necessary, clothing rather than limbs should be held, and if limbs have to be held this should be near the main joint such as the shoulder or hip. The patient can be controlled more easily if he is lying on a bed or on the floor, but pressure must not be applied to the neck, throat, chest or abdomen. Physical restraint should never be for a prolonged period and can usually be relaxed once additional drugs—by injection if necessary—take effect. Periods of isolation should have medical sanction and all incidents involving the use of restraint should be entered in writing in the daily nursing reports.

Disorders of sexual behaviour in adults
Persons with mental handicap have an immature personality and often a pattern of sexual behaviour appropriate to someone of a younger age. This immature pattern may persist into old age. Those who are severely handicapped may not show any sexual awareness even though some of the secondary sexual characteristics, such as menstruation, develop. In the handicapped adult male the external genitalia usually appear normal and, as with young adolescents, masturbation is common. This does not do harm to

the patient but care should be taken so that it does not take place in public or upset other people. Masturbation also occurs in the female but is less common and less obvious.

Homosexuality among handicapped males is usually an extension of masturbation but is sometimes of the kind seen in people of normal intelligence where one adopts the female role and the other the male. Strong emotional attachments with a sexual content may arise between female patients and can lead to very disturbed behaviour when it cannot be indulged, and in these cases it may be best to have the females live in different villas and only meet under supervision at activities in social clúbs, etc.

Sexual interest in young children is usually in the nature of curiosity and exhibitionism rather than an attempt to perform a sexual act, but when an adolescent or adult male shows sexual interest in a young child it is highly disturbing to the relatives and may be so to the child. Sexual interest in a girl also occurs because the mentally retarded male feels inferior in the company of a mature adult female. When this necessitates admission to hospital it is not usually difficult to arrange that contact with children is avoided except under supervision, but the abnormal desire may still be present after many years.

Incest is sexual intercourse between close relatives, most commonly between father and daughter. It may lead to hospital admission under a Court Order and, as this removes the mentally handicapped offender from the family, causes no special difficulties in hospital.

Rape is not common and the mentally handicapped offender usually goes to a special hospital (p. 138).

The sexually mature female with mental handicap may be very permissive and welcome any form of attention. She cannot be relied upon to practice any kind of birth control and apart from the risk of pregnancy runs a risk of contracting venereal disease. Both for her own protection and for the protection of others she may require to be admitted to hospital. These patients include some of the most difficult to care for. They may behave well for a time and then suddenly become disturbed. The good nurse learns from experience to observe when there is a change in mood and knows that extra attention and supervision are necessary until the patient settles. At times like this it may be advisable to deny the patient outdoor shoes and clothing so that it is more difficult for her to run away. These patients are usually 'high-grade' and may respond well to the responsibility of helping, under supervision, other patients who are severely subnormal, especially those with cerebral palsy or other physical handicap. This can satisfy an emotional need and earn them praise in a way which they have not had outside where they have been made to feel inferior.

10
Genetic Counselling

Parents and other relatives of mentally handicapped children want to know the risk of any subsequent children being similarly handicapped. Parents will also have wondered whether any one is to blame for the child being handicapped, whether any conduct or neglect during pregnancy, or at childbirth, has contributed to the handicap. Genetic counselling deals with these problems.

As a basis for genetic counselling it is important to try to make a diagnosis as to the cause of the abnormality. Some causes such as an infection of the brain, either before, or after birth, or brain damage due to lack of oxygen are unlikely to affect subsequent children, whereas when there is a known genetic condition there may be a high recurrence risk such as when one parent has tuberose sclerosis, or a lower risk of recurrence as where both parents are carriers for phenylketonuria. Most conditions are not as clear-cut as these, and even when the cause is known the recurrence risk may be quite small. Thus it is important to try to ascertain the cause, and where this cannot be found then to exclude the more likely inherited conditions.

11
Community Care

About 85 per cent of persons with mental handicap remain in the community and, as it is general policy to encourage this, special provisions are made to help their families. In Great Britain if frequent attention is required then the relatives providing this may qualify for a special *Attendance Allowance*, and where appropriate *Mobility Allowance*. Claim forms and explanatory leaflets are obtainable from any local social security office.

Where possible there should be a place of occupation outside of the home, during the day. This may be a:

Nursery school
Day care centre
School
Adult training centre
Sheltered workshop
Employment.

abcdefghijklm
ABC

Attendance at such centres will help to train and socialise the person and at the same time give the relatives a much needed rest. Most of these centres close at weekends and on public holidays, but at these times it is likely that the relatives will also be free from work and be able to give the necessary care.

The local authority through its education, and social service departments provides the special centres and it will depend on how ascertainment of the mental subnormality is made which department is contacted first.

Registration as a *Disabled Person* may help a handicapped person to get employment and at all times there should be special supervision to see that there is no commercial exploitation.

Hostels
For varying reasons, such as the demands of other children, old age, or a broken home some mentally handicapped people who would otherwise be able to stay at home cannot do so. For these there should be small hostels in the community where they can be looked after. Some hostels can be for those who have regular employment, whilst others may be linked to an occupation centre. It is sometimes advisable to have two or three hostels in a group to provide for different categories of handicapped people and to facilitate staffing. Where a hostel is associated with a hospital for mentally handicapped people it can be used

as a half-way house in which patients can be tried out before final discharge. On the other hand, should a need for greater care arise then admission to the hospital is more readily arranged.

Group homes and sheltered housing
In recent years, mentally handicapped persons have found accommodation in group homes, and also in sheltered housing projects. This form of living is suitable for fairly fit and able people who can be trained to do their own housekeeping. Successful group homes have been established for mentally handicapped people who have been suitably trained for discharge from hospital. Where satisfactory training has been provided, no residential staff is required in these homes (see p. 127). People in this kind of accommodation may be supervised by either Social Workers, or Community Nurses, or both.

Day Hospital
One or two hospitals run 'day hospitals' in the community and others admit on a daily basis mentally handicapped patients who are able to spend the night at home, but do not fit into the facilities provided by the local authorities.

Voluntary Associations
Parent groups and associations* can give much help, advice and moral support to the relatives of the mentally handicapped. Some of the associations have local branches and run social activities in the evenings and at weekends for handicapped persons, and at the same time these give the relatives an opportunity of discussing their problems amongst themselves. They also publish helpful explanatory booklets, list of accommodations etc., and organise larger meetings which can be used for publicity and for coordinating appeals for better facilities for the handicapped (p. 141).

*
See p. 141 for some names and addresses.

12

Hospital Care

Reasons for Admission to Hospital

Reasons which may require a patient to be admitted to hospital include:

Physical disability
Upset in development may affect the body as well as the mind and many babies who are severely handicapped are also paralysed. As a baby becomes older he grows heavier and more difficult to handle and this may make it impossible for normal family life to go on, especially where there are other children.

Chronic illness or disability developing later in life may also necessitate hospital admission.

Old age
This leads to physical deterioration and occurs in many of the mentally handicapped at an earlier age than usual.

Hyperkinetic behaviour
This is gross overactivity as a result of brain damage. The activity may be purposeless and destructive and the constant observation and control required is often more than can be given at home.

Epilepsy
Although most people with epilepsy are of normal intelligence epilepsy as the result of brain damage is common in mental handicap (p. 31).

Mental illness occurring together with mental handicap
The recognition of this is important for the mental illness may respond rapidly to treatment (p. 28).

Antisocial behaviour
This may be mainly confined to the home, or it may affect the general public. Sometimes it is no more than a frequent disturbance which makes normal family life impossible, and in other instances it is exemplified by irresponsible conduct with destruction of property, violence to persons or aberrant sexual behaviour. In such cases the admission to hospital may be the result of a Court Order (p. 137).

Hospital transfer
A mentally handicapped patient in another hospital may not be suitable for discharge, and if he is in an acute ward, as after a heart attack, or a surgical operation, then a direct transfer to a hospital for the mentally handicapped may be arranged.

Short-term admission for futher investigation or adjustment of drug therapy
This may be to allow certain laboratory tests to be carried out, or to provide skilled observation and assessment of the patient over a short period to determine whether there is in fact mental handicap and if so, whether prolonged hospital care is indicated.

Illness or death of relatives
The relatives who normally look after someone who has mental handicap may become unable to continue to do so through illness or death. If the illness is temporary then a short stay in hospital may suffice, but in other cases it becomes necessary because there is nowhere else suitable for them to go to.

Short-term admission to allow relatives to have a holiday

Unsuitable home
Whilst the patient's own home should provide more individual care than can be given in hospital a bad home can retard and disturb development. Then a period in hospital can help and may allow subsequent transfer to guardianship and a foster home or hostel.

Arranging Admission to a Hospital for the Mentally Handicapped

Patients with mental handicap may not themselves be able to understand the meaning of admission to hospital. Wherever possible the nearest relative or guardian should be concerned in the admission and agree to it. It is particularly important to obtain the cooperation of the relatives so that they can be encouraged to visit and take a continuing interest in the patient. If there should be sufficient improvement to justify discharge then the cooperation of the relatives will help in this.

In most cases admission should be arranged informally through:

1 The family doctor
2 Another hospital doctor (e.g. paediatrician or child psychiatrist)
3 An outpatient clinic where the patient may have been seen initially and been placed on a waiting list
4 A community hostel run in conjunction with a hospital where there is usually an arrangement for a hostel resident who requires greater care to be readily transferred to the hospital.

More formal admission under the Mental Health Act may be for:

Observation for up to 28 days
Treatment.

Admission under the Act may be at the request of the next of kin, or by a mental welfare officer, or it may be through the courts after an offence has been committed by the patient (pp. 137, 138).

The Environment in the Hospital

The newcomer to a hospital caring for the mentally handicapped will notice that much more living space is required for the patients than in a general hospital. Dayroom accommodation and occupational or recreational areas are far more important than the sleeping accommodation because, wherever possible, the patients are up during the day. Physical disabilities prevent many patients in hospital from negotiating stairs, so as much accommodation as possible should be on the ground floor. Ideally each ward should have direct access to open space. Small living units of no more than 30 adults or 20 children are much more suitable than large ones of perhaps up to 50 patients, as this makes it easier for the nursing staff to provide a 'home-like' atmosphere, but large wards are still common in quite a number of hospitals. Ventilation in dayrooms and dormitories requires particular attention as incontinence is a major factor in a hospital for the mentally handicapped.

Facilities
The following facilities should be provided in each living area:

A dayroom large enough to accommodate all the patients in the ward. This can be used for active play and should be equipped with record player and radio suitably installed so that the controls are out of the patients' reach.

A smaller dayroom with comfortable chairs where patients can sit quietly or watch television.

A dining room large enough to accommodate all patients at one sitting. The dining room will have to be cleaned after each meal and should not be relied upon as an additional dayroom.

A ward kitchen with a communicating serving counter to the dining room.

Storage space for linen, the patients' clothing, wheelchairs and other stores and ward equipment.

Dormitories and bedrooms. Dormitories should, preferably, have no more than six beds, except where the patients need a lot of supervision and then a larger dormitory is desirable. There should be one or two single rooms near the nurse's night station where patients can be isolated if they are unwell or are disturbing the others.

Each patient should have a bedside locker and chair. In addition, it is usually desirable to have a locker room where extra personal clothing and belongings may be kept.

Lavatories, bathrooms, and showers. These should be accessible for day and night use. Doors should be wide enough to allow room for wheelchairs and there should be enough space in the lavatory for a nurse in attendance. Locks on doors must be able to be opened from the outside.

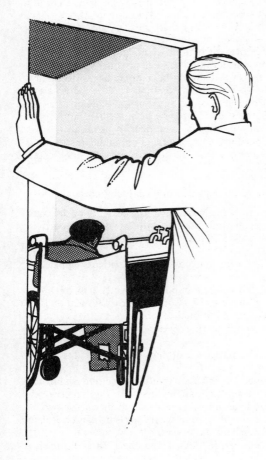

Showers are only suitable for patients who can attend to their own needs without the help of a member of staff.

A visitors' room where patients in the ward can see their relatives and friends. It should be large enough to accommodate about three patients and their visitors at any one time.

A clinical room in which medical examinations and essential nursing treatment can be carried out.

An office for the charge nurse. This can also be used for interviewing patients and relatives if there is no other room available for this purpose.

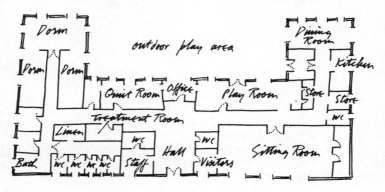

The office should have windows which allow observation of the dayrooms and dormitories. If the dormitories are upstairs, a nurse's station is required for the night staff.

A staff rest room with changing accommodation is required where the hospital is built on a house or villa pattern, as central facilities for the whole hospital would not be practicable.

Decor and furniture

Decor should be bright with colour schemes that are pleasing to the eye. Wall paintings or transfers add life and interest to otherwise bare surfaces and are more suitable than pictures which can get broken. There should be an adequate supply of mirrors at suitable levels so that patients approve their own image and learn to make the best of it. Paper posters may be hung, or pinned to the walls where poster boards are available. In children's wards a large writing surface for drawing and scribbling is useful. Walls and doors must all be washable.

Furniture requires to be strong and easily cleaned. Colours should be mixed to add variety and brighten the ward. The newer plastics, such as polypropylene, are not easily destroyed, but where fixed with screws to a metal frame the fixing screws must be secure. Legs of tables and chairs are potentially dangerous if the table or chair is overturned. Epileptic patients may require special chairs with a sloping back from which they cannot fall when they have a seizure.

Working, training, and recreational facilities
Apart from the ward units or villas the following facilities are found in many hospitals for mentally handicapped patients:

1 An area for pre-school sensory training of children
2 A school (if the hospital has patients of school age). It is run by the Education Authority
3 A training centre for adolescents who are too old to attend school
4 Occupational therapy department where arts and crafts are enjoyed by the patients and where vocational skills are also practised
5 Work therapy premises where the patients are taught simple assembly skills in preparation for working outside of the hospital

6 Department for sensory training and diversional therapy for adults

7 Hospital workshops; frequently used for the training of patients, as are farms and gardens which form part of quite a number of hospitals for mentally handicapped patients

8 Physiotherapy department

9 Assembly hall in which social activities take place; where church services can be held and films shown

10 Gymnasium for indoor sports activities and games

11 Swimming pool, which the patients enjoy under supervision

12 Social training for discharge.

Outdoor facilities

Outdoor recreational activities form part of most people's lives, and a hospital with large grounds is able to provide for its patients an active outdoor life in sunshine and fresh air.

Ideally, each ward or villa should have its own outdoor space with a play area, and an area for sitting and walking about in.

Some hospitals have rough grassland with trees where the patients may be taken for picnics. It must be remembered that it is not always easy to give all patients outings away from the hospital and those who are not able to be taken far away can still enjoy being out of doors.

Many hospitals have an adventure playground for the older children and adolescents. A sports ground gives many hours of enjoyment during

FIG 24

the summer, and some hospitals have a patients' football team.

Putting and bowling greens are appreciated by some of the patients as is the opportunity for helping to look after pets such as rabbits and guinea-pigs, and birds.

Visiting

This should be made as free as possible, but as most patients have some occupation during the day it is reasonable to recommend the most suitable times, so that visitors do not arrive when patients are away at their occupations. This is equally applicable to children going to the hospital school or training centres. Some patients cannot leave their ward areas so that facilities for visitors should be available at each ward. A central shop and tea room is desirable.

Fire precautions

Every nurse must familiarise herself with the local regulations. She must know where the nearest alarm points are and how to raise the alarm. After raising the alarm the first duty is to evacuate the patients. A list of patients should always be to hand so that a roll call can be made to ensure all patients have been evacuated.

Fire drill should be carried out regularly so that patients, as well as staff, know what to do when an alarm is given.

Procedure on Admission

Many hospitals have a separate admission unit to which all patients go initially so that any investigations and further assessment can be carried out before the patient is transferred to another area of the hospital. This has the advantage of allowing certain facilities, such as single rooms, laboratory equipment and the x-ray apparatus to be concentrated in the admission unit and it allows the staff there to be fully trained in the detailed procedure of admission. It may also make it easier for the patient to accept the fact of admission as this unit is more likely to resemble the popular idea of a hospital than the long-stay wards.

As soon as the admission to hospital of a patient has been arranged, the admission unit should be notified. It is important that the nurse in charge is fully prepared, so that on arrival the patient and relatives feel that they are expected and that they are receiving the unhurried attention of the staff.

Information prior to admission

Prior to the arrival of the patient the nurse in charge will want to know:

1 Name, age and sex of the patient and, if available, other data which allow her to prepare for the clerical part of the admission
2 The legal status of the patient, i.e. informal, under guardianship, on probation, or detained under a Court Order
3 Name, address and telephone number of next of kin, and of the family doctor
4 Details about the physical state of the patient, especially any disability which necessitates the use of special equipment, such as ripple bed, wheelchair, walking aid, etc.
5 The dietary needs of the patient so that a special diet can be ordered in readiness for the first meal the patient will have in the ward
6 Any known behaviour problems of the patient, or other special needs which may require extra staff on the ward. It is also helpful to know the local family words used for such things as toilet, etc.

If a single room is available which allows maximum observation by day and night, the patient should be admitted into it otherwise the bed in the dormitory should be close to the night nurse's station. Any special equipment needed should be placed ready for use. Only when the patient arrives on a stretcher should he be admitted straight into bed, otherwise he and the relatives should be shown into the visitors' room or into the charge nurse's office.

Information on admission

It is essential to get as much information as possible from the escorting relatives or officials. The patient can seldom be relied upon to give the information required.

The nurse's interview with the relatives

The first part of the interview is best conducted with both patient and relatives present and then such details as name, age, address, etc. can be verified, and the relatives can explain words used to indicate toilet requirements, favourite toys, etc. The main purpose of this part of the interview is to give the nurse a chance to observe the patient's behaviour in the presence of his relatives and the interaction between patient and relatives.

If the patient is mobile it is worthwhile showing him round the unit with the relatives so that his first acquaintance with his new surroundings is made while he still feels secure in the presence of his family. After this the patient can be handed over to the nurse who will bath him, while the nurse in charge continues the interview with the next of kin and takes any further details about the family history, the patient's behaviour, abilities, etc. It is valuable if she can also form an opinion of the relatives' attitudes towards the patient and his handicap so that she can make a rough assessment of how much continuing interest and cooperation can be expected. The relatives should be encouraged to express any fears or worries they may have. Visiting hours and procedures about holidays, food parcels, etc. should be explained to the relatives. Regulations as to smoking and the undesirability of giving matches or lighters to the patients should be emphasised.

Many hospitals have a standard form to be completed either before, or on admission. This form is intended to obtain as much information as possible about the present and past history of the patient and includes such questions as:

Present history
Ability to feed
Any kinds of food to avoid
Ability to dress and wash
Has he adequate vision (? spectacles)
Has he adequate hearing (? hearing aid)
Ability to talk and make his needs known
Ability to walk, especially on stairs
Sleeping habits
Bowel habits
Menstrual history
Epilepsy? Yes/No. If so, kind of seizure and whether any warning
General behaviour: friendly; withdrawn; noisy; destructive, etc.
Details of any drug therapy
Details of any drug allergies
General level of intelligence with results of any tests.

Previous history
Age when retardation first noticed
Any serious illness
Particulars of vaccinations and inoculations
Details of previous schooling
Details of previous employment.

Family history
Health of mother during pregnancy
Duration of pregnancy
Obstetric history
Mother's age at birth
Ages and sexes of siblings
Any history of similar abnormalities in relatives.

After the admission procedure is finished the relatives should say good-bye to the patient so that they may depart for home. It is wise to make certain that the relatives have told the patient that he will stay behind. Great distress can be caused if the relatives depart without saying that they are going and whether and when they will return for a visit. A patient who feels he has been abandoned or kept against his will, will try to get home without permission, and this makes the supervision of the patient all the more difficult.

Observation of the patient during admission
The nurse who takes the new patient to the bath will have to observe him carefully so that she can add her report to the admission notes. Her observations broadly fall into three categories:

1 *Physical state*
   Body build and general state of nutrition: degree of cleanliness of body and clothes. Signs of suspected scabies, or of head, body or pubic lice. Presence of scars, bruises, swellings, skin rashes, scratch marks and deformities.

2 *Physical ability*
   The degree to which he moves about, helps to undress, how much help he needs to get into the bath, and any other observations which can serve as a starting point towards planning the care of the patient.

3 *Mood and behaviour*
   An assessment should also be made of the patient's mood; his behaviour should be noted including his interaction with the nurse.

While these observations are made the patient is bathed and put to bed for examination by the doctor. The patient's cooperation is gained as far as possible by simple explanation. A nurse who has gained his cooperation is likely to be the best person to assist during the medical examination.

Medical examination

The functions of the nurse during the examination are:

The comforting and reassuring of the patient
The preparing of equipment as necessary
Assisting the medical staff
Arranging for specimens to be sent to the laboratory.

Two nurses may be needed if the patient is completely helpless, or if he is uncooperative.

Prior to the doctor's arrival the nurse will have:

Measured the patient's height and weight
Recorded the pulse rate
Recorded the rate of respiration
Recorded the body temperature.

Additional examinations and assessment

X-ray examination

X-ray examinations of the chest, skull or other parts of the body may be ordered. The nurse will have to make sure that transport is arranged for the patient should this be necessary, that any preparation of the patient prior to the examination has been carried out, that he is suitably dressed, and that an escort is available.

Dental examination

Regular dental examinations are necessary and it is appropriate that the newly admitted patient has a check-up soon after admission. Unless the need is urgent this should be postponed until the patient has settled in. The nurse accompanies the patient to the dental treatment room and stays with him during the examination.

Psychological examination

Psychological testing and assessment can be made after a few weeks once the patient has fully settled into his new surroundings. It is important that the patient should be in a quiet cooperative mood when this is done, and therefore the nurse should see that, if possible, no upsets occur before the testing. Some patients are easily upset at certain times of the day, and in that case the appointment must be made for a time when the patient is at his best. The patient should have had a meal or snack before the appointment so that he is not hungry, and should have visited the lavatory. Should he have had a seizure, or be upset or aggressive for some reason, then the appointment should be cancelled.

As the various examinations and investigations are carried out a treatment and care plan for the patient is worked out. The nurse contributes to the formulation of this plan by the report she presents after admission, and later at the case conference she attends.

The introduction of the new patient to the other patients in the unit should be done at a time when quiet activities are going on so that the newcomer is not alarmed about the noise and bustle. The patient who came from a quiet family where those around him understood his wants and ways can be frightened when he meets a number of new people

whose words and gestures he does not easily understand. This applies especially if the admission unit is large. The nurse must be aware of this and make certain that the new patient is always supervised so that upsets and aggressive outbursts are avoided.

Ward rules may not have much meaning to the patient but it is worthwhile introducing them step by step to see how far they are understood.

Standards of behaviour should be laid down from the outset and agreed lines adhered to.

Care of Patients' Property

Most patients derive some comfort from having personal possessions around them when they come into hospital. This applies not only to their own clothing, but also to such things as favourite toys. The possession of personal items should be encouraged as it helps the new patient to settle into his new surroundings. At the same time, however, it must be explained to the relatives that it may not be possible to guarantee the safe-keeping of such items since they may get lost or destroyed.

Valuable items should be discouraged as the financial value is seldom appreciated by the patient who may place more importance on glitter, size or texture. Safe-keeping is always a problem and, whilst valuables may be given to the Hospital Secretary for safe-keeping (and a receipt obtained), most wards require a lock-fast cupboard where property can be kept overnight, or at weekends, or when a patient is in a disturbed or destructive phase. Bed-side lockers are useful in most wards, but do not always lock. It must be remembered that some patients with mental handicap have little regard for other people's property and will go into other patients' lockers unless closely supervised. If there are many such patients it may be necessary to have a locked locker room outside the dormitory with the keys kept by the nursing staff.

At the time of admission items of personal property are listed and the list kept up to date. Money and other valuables can either be returned to the next of kin and a receipt obtained, or placed in the hospital safe.

Similarly a list must be made of all articles of clothing returned to the relatives, and a receipt should be obtained. All clothing retained will have to be marked with the patient's name and entered into the clothing sheet which is signed by the relatives. It must be explained to them that any articles of personal clothing taken home or brought into hospital in the future must be recorded on the clothing sheet if the nursing staff are to be held responsible for them.

13

Patient Care

General Considerations

A basic routine to regulate the main activities in a day is always necessary where groups of people live together. Even in the normal family mealtimes and other activities follow a regular pattern which is only broken when special events occur.

Hospital routine must meet the needs of the patients and at the same time allow for the coordination of the various hospital departments which, directly or indirectly, contribute to patient care.

If we remember that handicapped patients are admitted to hospital because they are unable to meet the varying demands of daily living, then we will appreciate that a simple daily routine helps them to adjust to the best of their ability. Routine brings order into life, and a calm and orderly atmosphere aids in establishing a feeling of security and safety. We all know that small children become irritable and upset when breaks in routine disturb their regular feeding and sleeping habits because they cannot understand the reasons for this. In the same way the mentally handicapped find it easier to understand and follow a regular pattern of living in which certain events, such as getting up, washing, feeding, etc. always follow each other in the same order. Even some quite severely handicapped patients can, when encouraged in a calm and unstressful atmosphere over a long period of time, learn to perform simple tasks such as washing, dressing and feeding themselves.

Routine must not be confused with regimentation. Routine should provide the conditions in which each patient gets the opportunity to develop to his maximum. In a regimented atmosphere tasks are done, not because they are in the interests of the patient but because they suit the institution and therefore it is important that routine procedures are reviewed regularly to see if it is still in the patient's best interest to continue them.

It is of fundamental importance in the caring of the mentally handicapped that the nurse and other members of staff should learn the usual pattern of behaviour of each patient. Many patients with mental handicap do not conform to the pattern of behaviour expected by society in a person of their age. The behaviour which they exhibit is more appropriate to their mental age and the older a child grows the greater become the differences between his real age and his mental age.

Many severely handicapped patients in hospital cannot speak and if something is upsetting them then it is only by the intelligent observation of changes in their usual pattern of behaviour that the nurse knows to look for the cause of the change. Again some severely handicapped patients do not appear to feel, or react to, pain as much as a normal person. Pain serves a protective function in alerting a person to illness. A surgical emergency such as acute appendicitis or a perforated duodenal ulcer may go unnoticed where the patient either does not, or cannot complain of pain. Broken bones may not be complained of and only noticed when the nurse realises that a limb is not being used normally. The nurse must be an interpreter for her patient.

In normal society a person has a home, a job and various kinds of recreation where he will meet with different people. So also in hospital there should be groupings for residence, for occupation and for recreation. It may sometimes be necessary to separate adults from children, and when male and female patients are together, adequate supervision will be required. There must be facilities to isolate a patient temporarily if his behaviour becomes too outrageous (see Ch. 9).

Meals and Feeding

Meal times occupy an important part of a patient's life in hospital and should be made an enjoyable social activity. The general surroundings and the presentation of the food should be made as attractive as possible.

Supervision of the patient's meals is the responsibility of the nursing staff. In addition to the feeding of patients and the teaching of good eating habits, this also includes the serving of meals and the supervision of the domestic staff in relation to the handling of food on the ward and the cleanliness of the ward kitchen and dining room premises.

Basic dietary needs
Adult patients who are active have the same dietary needs as the normal adult and should receive a balanced diet containing such protein foods as meat, fish, eggs and cheese: carbohydrates such as bread, cereals, cakes, sugar and jam: fresh fruit and vegetables in season: and about ½ pint of milk daily which can be given in drinks and puddings. Fats will be given as butter or margarine and in the cooking; vitamin and iron supplements may be ordered if the patients require these.

Adolescents and older children have similar basic requirements to adults but should be given extra protein in the form of milk and eggs, and may require larger portions at mealtimes to satisfy their needs while they are still growing.

Basic meals are prepared in central hospital kitchens and transferred to the wards or villas in heated trolleys. If a choice of menu is offered it is fairly easy to cater for the individual patient's likes and dislikes. If there is no choice then the nurse will have to notify the kitchen and order an alternative meal when a patient persistently refuses food because he does not like it.

Small babies will be bottle fed until they are ready to be weaned and start mixed feeding.

Special dietary needs
Special dietary needs exist in a number of patients either because food has to be prepared in special ways, or because certain foods have to be provided in definite quantities or because certain foods have to be excluded. Examples of such diets are:

1 *The semi-solid diet*
This diet is required for patients who have difficulty in chewing or swallowing solid food. It differs from the basic diet in consistency but not in quantity or quality. Meat is given in the form of minced beef, lamb, chicken, etc. and potatoes and vegetables are mashed. A semi-solid diet can be supplied as such from the central kitchen ready for serving; but nowadays many wards have a liquidiser installed so that the food can be prepared on the ward. It must be remembered that, although the patient requires soft food, it should be attractive to look at, and therefore meat, vegetables and potatoes should be prepared separately. Fresh fruit is similarly prepared for the patient.

2 *The obesity diet*
An obesity diet is prescribed for patients who are significantly overweight. It is designed to lower the total food intake to such an extent that the patient will have to use some of his own accumulated fat stores to meet his energy needs. The diet will be prepared by the dietician, and to the ward will be sent the food that the patient is allowed to eat. It is important to remember that no extras must be given to the patient, and that the foods which are most severely restricted are often those which are taken as snacks between mealtimes, or can be bought at the shop by the patients themselves, e.g. sweets, biscuits, cakes, etc. Vitamin and mineral supplements are sometimes ordered for patients whose diet is restricted while they are reducing their weight.

3 *The diabetic diet*
Diabetes mellitus is a disorder in which the cells of the body are to a greater or lesser degree unable to utilise the sugar in the bloodstream which is mainly derived from carbohydrate foods. This is due to the total or partial absence of a hormone called insulin which is made in the pancreas. In severe cases insulin is given by injection to the

patient; in milder cases oral drugs can be used. Sometimes it is possible to control the disease by diet alone.

The prescribed diet is designed to meet the individual patient's needs and will vary from person to person. The young diabetic patient who is receiving insulin will have a fairly liberal diet in quantity, although the various foods used are strictly controlled; whereas the obese, less active, or elderly patient will receive a diet restricted in carbohydrate content and reduced in quantity which will also enable his weight to be brought down to a normal level. The diet is ordered by the physician and prepared in the kitchen by a dietician who will supply the ward with the meal the patient requires. The nurse will have to make sure that the patient eats what is prescribed, especially when insulin is used, and that he has no additional foods from any other sources. However, apples, oranges and diabetic fruit juices may be allowed in moderation. The patient's likes and dislikes regarding food should be made known to the dietician so that he is not served with meals that he is not prepared to eat. If, for some reason, a patient is not able to take a meal, he should be given a glucose drink, and this is especially important when the patient is being given insulin.

Mentally handicapped patients who are diabetic and on insulin should have their urine tested at least twice daily, and sometimes more often. Special observation is needed when the urine is completely free of sugar to watch for any tendency towards too low a blood sugar (hypoglycaemia).

4 *Other special requirements*

Occasionally the nurse may meet patients who have special dietary requirements, such as patients with liver or heart diseases, or patients who suffer from allergic reactions to certain foods. Special diets may be required in cases of rare metabolic disorders, such as phenylketonuria (p. 24). The hospital kitchen will supply these special diets and details of such diets can be studied in textbooks dealing with nutrition.

Preparation for Meals

The ward kitchen

The ward kitchen should be large enough to accommodate the heated meal trolley which transports the food from the central kitchen to the ward. A thermostatically controlled warming cupboard is desirable to ensure that plates are warmed but not too hot to hold. There should be cupboard space for crockery and cutlery required on the ward and all extra food in the ward should be stored in the kitchen. A refrigerator should be available for the storage of milk, butter and other perishable items. There should be facilities for making tea and other hot drinks and for preparing bread and butter and small snacks.

Washing up facilities should include a stainless steel sink unit, preferably with a waste disposal unit. This is a useful hygienic method of disposing of food left over by the patients. Dish washing machines may either be of the domestic type with a cycle of about thirty minutes for a complete wash and dry, or of the commercial type which are much quicker and so can deal with more dishes in a shorter time.

Dry stores such as tea, sugar and coffee are best kept in airtight plastic or metal containers and jam, marmalade, syrup etc. in glass jars. Bread, cakes and biscuits should be kept in separate tins or plastic containers.

Food bought personally by the patients or brought in by relatives for individual use should also be kept in the kitchen rather than in the patient's locker in the dormitory. For high-grade patients individual plastic boxes labelled with the patient's name should be available from which the patient can help himself. Low-grade patients and all other patients who cannot be trusted to eat with discretion from their personal stores will have to have their snacks allocated to them at the appropriate times. It is important to see that food is not secreted in dormitories and other places where it will attract mice, or where patients on diets can find it.

Before each meal, dishes and cutlery should be taken from the kitchen and the places in the dining area set out. Jugs of milk and water should be taken in last so that they are not left sitting on the tables uncovered. Serving spoons should be laid out in the kitchen, plates put to heat if needed, and all other preparations made, such as buttering bread, etc.

Patients are sometimes involved in the activities taking place in ward kitchens and dining rooms as part of their training programme or as part of the employment programme. The initial teaching and supervision of patients during their training programme is part of nursing care and should only be handed over to the domestic staff when a stage of training is reached where the patient requires no more than routine supervision. In the interests of the prevention of spreading of food-borne infections it is wiser not to allow patients unsupervised access to kitchen premises.

The dining room or dining area
Wherever possible, a special room or part of a room should be set aside in which all the patients who are out of bed and able to sit at table can have their meals. This space should not also be used for other activities so that it may be prepared and cleared in good time.

The room should be attractive, clean and well ventilated. If space allows, small tables are desirable as patients may then be separated into

small groups of four. Patients with special problems or on diets can sit together. Tables for four are also ideal where wheelchairs are brought in to the dining room.

Table tops should be made of a material which does not show stains and which can be cleaned easily. Hard, heat resistant plastic surfaces are excellent in this respect and are widely used, and can be obtained in several different colours. Table cloths are seldom used nowadays; this is partly a question of economy and partly one of fashion. Sometimes where a smooth table top makes it impossible for the patient to control his plate a type of plastic table cloth which is easily wiped clean after the meal, or table mats, can be provided. These are available in many attractive designs and colours. Another alternative is to use a suction pad on the bottom of the plate.

Chairs should be of a convenient height to allow the patient to reach the table easily. High chairs for children may be needed or, alternatively,

low tables provided for all patients who cannot easily reach the table. Feeding trays may be used for certain patients who are in wheelchairs.

Preparation of the patients
Where necessary, patients should be toileted before meals and all should have washed their hands. Any activities preceding a meal should be quiet ones so that the patients are not overexcited and perspiring when they enter the dining room. All those on training programmes should be inspected before entering the dining room to see if they fulfil the standard laid down in their programme, as for instance tidiness of dress, change of shoes, face shaved, etc. and they should be sent back if necessary.

Everybody should be seated before the meal is served and remain seated until the meal is over. An exception might be made with patients on a diet, especially with those who are reducing their weight, and who may either feed before other patients or be allowed to leave before the sweet course is served so that they are not tempted to help themselves to the portions of other patients.

The nurses should note and report if a patient leaves significant amounts of food on the plate and, if necessary, give help to those who have difficulties in managing their meal. A senior nurse should be responsible for giving out the food including second helpings to ensure that extra food is not given to those who should not get it.

Patients who require to be fed or who are being trained to feed themselves may have their meals at the same time as the other patients, providing their number is small and enough nurses are on duty to undertake the feeding and training, as well as the serving, of the other patients. If not, these patient may have their meal either before or after the others as the ward routine allows.

Sometimes high-grade patients help with the serving of meals as part of their training programme. Any patients involved in this activity should complete their own meals before they start serving others.

Self-feeding training

As soon as a patient reaches the stage of development when he can sit unsupported and begins to reach for nearby objects it is time to introduce training in self-feeding. Some spilling and messiness is inevitable and plastic bibs with a container at the foot are useful. These are also made in adult sizes.

Drinking from a cup can be introduced as soon as the patient can safely pick it up, put it to his mouth and tilt and return it to the table. A baby's feeding cup weighted at the bottom so that it rights itself and with a non-spill top can be used to start with until the patient develops enough muscular coordination to return the cup to the table without upsetting it. Later an ordinary cup should be used.

Spoonfeeding requires much more skill, as only one hand can be used to control the spoon which has to be filled and carried from plate to mouth without losing too much of the food. For the beginner semi-solid food is easier and a baby's plate may be used which has a deep rim and a small suction pad underneath to fix it to the table and stop it from sliding. The patient can then concentrate on the use of the spoon only. Soups should only be given when good hand-eye coordination has developed and when the patient no longer loses food from the spoon. At this stage it is time to introduce an ordinary plate so that the patient uses the other hand to steady it. Spoon and pusher combined may be tried when the patient is able to feed with the spoon alone and manages his plate without the use of the other hand. With patience and perseverance the most able patients will eventually learn to cut up their food and use fork and knife, but in many this level of skill will not be reached.

It must be remembered that during the initial stages of training the patient's ability should not be over-estimated nor the exercise prolonged beyond the stage after which the patient will do without food rather than struggle. It may be necessary to finish the meal by feeding to ensure a sufficient intake of food.

Some patients who have spent some years of their lives at home in the care of relatives are unable to feed themselves when admitted to hospital or hostel because they have been fed at home. Learning to feed can be a

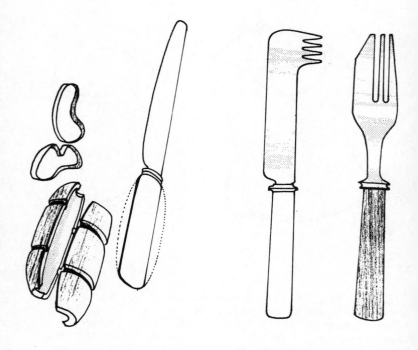

prolonged messy business and some mothers clearly prefer to feed their handicappped child rather than train him to learn because it takes less time to feed than to teach. In such patients a feeding programme should be started as soon after admission as the patient has settled in.

The teaching of good table manners is important and is introduced side by side with training in self-feeding.

Patients with Special Food Problems

Care of the patient who vomits or regurgitates food

A number of low-grade patients habitually vomit or regurgitate food and make it very difficult to ensure adequate nutrition and maintenance of their weight. Great patience is needed when feeding to ensure that at least some of the food stays down. Glucose drinks and high calorie foods may be given. Weighing should be done weekly to check that the patient is not losing ground.

It is also important that in addition to cleansing the mouth, vomited or regurgitated material is cleaned from the skin at once to prevent excoriation of the lower face and neck.

Care of the obese patient
Overweight patients who are on a reducing diet must be observed carefully to prevent them from eating extra food. They may not understand the reason for the dietary restrictions imposed on them and they might try to obtain something to eat whenever they are hungry. During mealtimes they should sit together with other patients who are on a diet so that they can be supervised. If possible, three or four patients on a reducing diet may be grouped together and their day planned in such a way that they have little opportunity for breaking their diet. Their weight should be checked weekly and recorded. Attractive clothing promised for wearing when they are slimmer might serve as an incentive. (Relatives, as well as the hospital shop, must be informed so that they can cooperate.)

The care of the diabetic patient
The diabetic patient requires special mention. Constant supervision will be needed to make sure that nothing in addition to the prescribed diet is eaten and the cooperation of relatives and friends must be sought so that they will not supply the patient with extra food. The hospital shop should have a list of the names of all diabetic patients and should stock such things as diabetic chocolate and fruit juices which the patients may purchase and eat as part of their diet.

14
Clothing

The provision of the right type of clothing for large numbers of patients with a variety of special needs, usually with limited resources of money, is a problem which every hospital for the mentally handicapped has to solve. The general aim, whether the clothing is bought by the hospital or by the patients themselves, is to have each patient suitably and smartly dressed and to provide variety in the types of clothing with a selection of styles and colours and with some regard to fashion. It must be comfortable and non-constricting, and on the whole easily put on with the fastenings at the front as far as possible. Patients who continually remove their clothes may have the fastenings at the back. It should be durable and hard-wearing despite abuse, and it must be washable without losing its shape or colour in the process. The clothing should also be reasonably priced. The nurse must be aware of these considerations if she is to assist in the task of meeting the patients' needs.

Basic Clothing Needs

A large number of handicapped patients are up and about all day, engaged in work and recreational activities and their clothing needs correspond in many ways to those of the average individual. Their basic clothing requirements can be listed as follows, but quantities will depend on the frequency of laundry service:

The adult male
>   4 sets of underwear
>   4 pairs of socks
>   6 shirts and ties
>   2 pullovers
>   2 cardigans
>   1 suit for special occasions
>   1 leisure suit, or trousers and jacket or blazer
>   1 winter coat, or dufflecoat
>   1 raincoat
>   1 anorak, with hood
>   2 pairs of shoes
>   1 pair of slippers
>   3 pairs of pyjamas
>   Handkerchiefs
>   Working clothes as required: overalls, boots, etc.

All these items of clothing should be labelled with the patient's name and he should be encouraged to care for them as far as possible. He should have wardrobe space allocated to himself, and also a drawer where he can store his things. He should be taken to be fitted when his clothes are bought and, if necessary, alterations should be made to ensure a good fit. It is often difficult to buy clothes 'off-the-peg' as the physique of many handicapped patients does not correspond to stock sizes, and separate jacket and trousers are better than a badly fitting suit. When possible clothing should be of flame-proof material.

The same applies to females whose basic requirements are:

The adult female

    6 sets of underwear, to include vest, bra', pants and slip
    4 pairs of tights, or stockings and a 'liberty bodice' or corset
    4 dresses for summer and winter wear
    2 skirts   } only if the patient can wear these; many
    2 blouses } handicapped females look better in dresses
    2 pullovers
    2 cardigans
    1 winter coat
    1 raincoat and hat
    1 anorak, with hood
    2 pairs of shoes
    1 pair of slippers
    3 nightdresses or pairs of pyjamas
    2 aprons
    Handkerchiefs
    Working clothes if required, including overalls and shoes.

Children

The basic needs here are more difficult to list as they vary according to age, but the active child of school age would require most of the items listed for adults, possibly with additional sets of underwear and extra shirts and dresses. Special care must be taken with growing children to ensure that nylon socks and tights, as well as shoes, fit well and are not too tight.

Special Clothing Needs

A large number of handicapped persons have special needs regarding clothing and shoes which have to be met on an individual basis, and a great deal of ingenuity is often required to adapt materials and styles to overcome their problems. The main categories that can be listed here are the following.

The incontinent

The incontinent adult patient, and the older child, who is up and about present a very special problem regarding clothing. The total number of changes needed during the day may be as many as ten or twelve, and a large stock of clothing is required. Under these circumstances it is often difficult to provide individually allocated clothing and there is a tendency to carry a general stock of suitable clothing which the patients then share. Especially is this so at weekends and holidays when the laundry is closed and washing facilities are not available.

Protective undergarments in the form of waterproof pants for the incontinent should be used whenever possible, and absorbent pads have a place in the nursing of those patients who pass small amounts of urine frequently.

Trousers for the incontinent male patient must be made of strong material which can survive many washings. Man-made fibres like Terylene for trousers are suitable; strong cotton materials are sometimes used to make quick-change trousers for patients in the wards.

For the incontinent female patient skirts and blouses are more suitable than dresses as this makes changing easier. Crimplene and cotton materials are best suited for making skirts.

The destructive patient

A few patients are so disturbed that they tear almost any type of clothing that is put on them. This can be very expensive and sometimes an outfit does not last longer than a few days. Clothing for this type of patient must be made of very strong material, such as strong nylon or even canvas; it must be simply sewn with as few seams as possible and with all fastenings at the back out of the patient's reach.

Patients with problems of locomotion

The 'toe-walker'

A small group of patients have the habit of walking on their toes only. They tend to go about without shoes and the result is that they wear out their socks very quickly. The socks slip down and a portion of the sock dangles in front of them which makes walking dangerous. Well-fitting socks with elastic at the ankles to keep them up are most suitable for these patients, and it is possible to re-inforce the part of the sock used for walking so that it lasts longer.

The 'crawler'

A few patients are unable to walk but they manage to move about the floor using either their knees or the seat of their pants. This is very hard on the clothes, especially when the patient is mobile enough to move around the room or garden. Here it helps if leather patches can be sewn over those parts of the clothing that are exposed to wear and tear.

Patients' Private Clothing

Ideally every patient should have his or her own clothes, carefully marked with the name and reserved for his or her use only. Unfortunately, this is not always possible especially where the patient is destructive or incontinent. Newly admitted patients, particularly when they are able to appreciate personal belongings, derive comfort and pleasure from wearing their own things. Relatives can be encouraged to include items of clothing in the gifts they bring to the patients when they visit and also for birthdays and Christmas gifts.

Patients who have saved, or been given, money can have clothing purchased for their own use. A shopping expedition under the care of a nurse gives the patient a chance to choose according to taste, with the nurse making sure that the choice is suitable and within the patient's means.

Some hospitals have arrangements with shops or clothing firms who provide 'sheltered' shopping opportunities. This is especially suitable for patients who would otherwise not be able to go out. In some instances a store may open in the evening particularly for the patients who, escorted by nurses, can then make their purchases; or a firm may accept an invitation to bring a selection of clothing to the hospital and set up a store for one or two days. Large hospitals with a number of fairly helpless patients find this arrangement very satisfactory.

A list must be kept of all clothing personally owned by patients, and this should be kept up-to-date by adding any items that have been acquired and removing worn out or outgrown clothes which have to be discarded. All alterations in the clothing record should be countersigned by another nurse.

Choice of socks, stockings, and shoes

Socks and stockings may either be brought in by the patient's relatives or supplied by the hospital. Ideally, every patient should have his own supply, but it is often very difficult, especially in wards with a large number of patients, to mark socks and stockings individually.

Socks and stockings should be inspected at night and sent to the laundry regularly. Clean socks should be laid out, either the patient's own marked with his name, or a pair from stock which will fit. It is important to see that socks are not too small, as nylon socks do not have much 'give' and too small a size would cramp the toes and cause fatigue.

Stretch socks overcome this problem to some extent, but even with these selection of the right size is important, as otherwise the socks tend to slip down at the heel. Every effort should be made to encourage the patients to have their own socks or stockings and keep them in their lockers or cupboards.

Shoes must be fitted individually, not only to the correct size but also to the right width. Patients with deformities of the feet or abnormalities of gait should be especially fitted, and insoles may be needed. Orthopaedic shoes may be supplied for some patients. Slip-on shoes are often preferred to lace-up shoes, as nurses often find that the laces are badly tied, or completely lost, leaving the patient shuffling about and liable to stumble.

Dressing and Undressing

Persistent effort and much patience on the part of the nurses are required to teach handicapped patients to dress and undress themselves. Poor balance, imperfect muscular coordination when trying to perform complicated movements and the tendency to do things hastily are only some of the difficulties that patients have in taking off and putting on their clothes, and it may take many weeks or months before a patient has acquired even some degree of perfection.

A number of complicated tasks require to be mastered by the patient when learning to dress and undress. There is first of all the problem of getting articles of clothing over the head and into the arms, taking off pants and putting them on, getting socks and shoes onto feet, and the difficult job of putting on a jacket or cardigan. Here the patient will have to start with simple tasks, the nurse encouraging and helping all the time when necessary, the patient thus gradually becoming more and more skilful. It may take months or years before the complexity of tying laces and ties, and the fastening of buttons and zips is mastered. Clothes which fasten at the front or side are more suitable than those which fasten at the back. Velcro may sometimes be used in place of buttons and zip fasteners.

Additionally, the patient has to learn the difference between back and front, the inside and outside of a garment, and also which articles of clothing come first and which last. Good ward organisation and team work will make this easier for both patients and nurses. If name tapes are brightly coloured and always sewn on the same place, the patient will find it easier to distinguish back from front, and the inside from the outside of a garment.

Cooperation between the nurses who get the patient up in the morning and those who put him to bed at night can ensure that clothes are always folded in the same way and put into bundles always in the same order. When the patient is ready he should help to lay out and fold the clothes and develop the habit of tidiness. It is very important to discourage from the outset any activities which are likely to develop into bad habits. Clothes taken off should not be stood on, or thrown about. Full attention should be given to the job in hand and the patient should be stopped from running about as this interrupts his own activities and disturbs others.

The nurse should talk to the patient, helping him to identify garments by name, and encouraging him to respond. A lot of praise is needed, even when progress is painfully slow. Scolding should be avoided when the patient finds progress difficult; it never helps and only produces a feeling of uselessness on the part of the patient which leads to frustration. Tears and tantrums result and both patient and nurse may give up trying.

Shoes, slippers and footwear in general present a special problem, as so many handicapped patients find it very difficult to distinguish between left and right. In female footwear one often finds buckles or buttons on the outer side of the shoes, so that these can be used as an aid for the patient, for instance by saying, 'stand your shoes together, and your feet together; if the shoes are the right way, you have the buttons outside'.

Laces and buckles are difficult to fasten as so many patients lack the degree of muscular coordination and steadiness required to do this. Even those who could do this task, if they spent sufficient time on it, often get fed up and leave the shoes undone, or struggle in and out of their shoes without unfastening them, thus treading down the backs. In these instances it might be advisable to see that the patients get slip-on shoes to wear.

Many of the patients can eventually with encouragement learn to appreciate the finer points of dressing. The provision of a full-length mirror allows them to notice the correct position of zip fasteners in skirts, the straightness of the tie, etc. They can also learn when it is necessary to change dirty clothes, and may from there progress to taking complete care of their wardrobes, including selecting their clothes, laying them out, and washing and drying their 'smalls'.

Since the ability to dress and undress is such an important step towards independence it is essential that every patient is encouraged to progress as far as he can possibly go, even if it takes years to achieve results.

15

Personal Care

This chapter outlines the personal care which a nurse is expected to give to a mentally handicapped patient. It is equally of value to parents, relatives and non-nursing care staff.

The physical welfare of patients is in the nurse's hands. She alone with her patience and skill can see to it that patients are comfortable in every way. One of the biggest problems in any hospital situation can be the care and supervision of the patient's skin and this applies even more in a mental handicap hospital when the patient's condition prevents normal patient/nurse cooperation.

When a patient is admitted the nursing records must include information about the condition of the patient's skin. Routine inspection of the skin should be made whenever the patient has a bath, when he returns from visits outside the hospital, however brief, and when he returns from sports events or any other activities where he might have injured himself.

When inspecting the skin, the nurse should routinely look for, and report in the nurse's notes, any abnormalities seen.

Daily Care

Washing

Washing of face and hands should be routine for all patients first thing in the morning and before going to bed at night. After visiting the lavatory the hands should be washed, and this should also be routine before meals are served. Patients who are fit to go to work or school, or who attend the various therapy classes should be trained and encouraged to wash their hands and faces when they return to the ward.

Soap and towels should be available near all the washhand basins that the patients use. Disposable towels are most suitable here as this avoids the problem of patients fetching their own towels and mixing them up. Good supervision is needed so that the soap and towels do not get wasted.

For bed patients the bathing trolley may be used and the nurse should remember to change the water between each patient.

The soap supplied to the patients for this purpose should be toilet soap, either in the form of a cake of soap, or liquid soap in a dispenser. Household washing soap is not suitable as it is too harsh for the skin. Many patients do not have normal skin; sometimes it is very dry, as in

Down's syndrome, or very greasy, and unsuitable soap may irritate an already abnormal skin.

Bathing
Cleanliness of the skin is essential in community living. Ideally, every patient should have a bath each day. However, this is not often possible, but where patients are able enough to look after themselves with only a minimum of supervision, the opportunity to have a quick bath or shower is appreciated. A weekly bath is the minimum that any ward or hostel should allow for. Most patients are bathed more frequently, and those who are incontinent may require a bath more often than once daily.

Bathing may be done in a shower, if the patient is capable of caring for his own person. Wards which have recently been built or up-graded are generally equipped with showers. Showers are not suitable for patients who require assistance and should not be used in those instances.

Bathing in the bath is suitable for most patients. Patients who are well and able may be allowed to look after themselves. Others may need varying degrees of help, and even severely handicapped and crippled patients can be bathed in this way if sufficient assistance is given.

A small number of patients will have to be bathed in bed. Those who are acutely ill, or so severely handicapped that it is impossible to take them to the bathroom in a chair or on a trolley, will require a bedbath.

Shower baths
Although patients may be fit to have a shower bath without assistance, there are several points the nurse must not ignore. The shower should be inspected to make sure that:

1 It is safe, clean and ready for use
2 A non-slip mat is in place
3 The water tap is adjusted to the right temperature (38°C).

All showers must be fitted with mixer taps so that the patient cannot make the temperature of the water too hot.

Check that the patient has with him all he requires:

1 Change of clothing, either night clothes if the shower is last thing at night, or day clothes if in the morning
(Female patients will need a plastic shower cap.)
2 Soap and face cloth
3 Bath towel
4 Chair.

Please remember that although the patient may be able to attend to his own needs he is still your responsibility. Make sure you always know when a patient is having a shower and that the door is not locked. Access to the patient is necessary and you may have to inspect his body for rashes, bruises, etc. if he has returned from leave, or has just been admitted.

The bathroom
Inspect the bathroom and see that it is clean and ready for use. The window should be closed to avoid draughts. There should be a non-slip mat and a chair. *When not in use the bathroom door should be kept locked at all times.*

In most hospitals for handicapped patients the bath taps are fitted with mixer taps. These are turned on with a key. The care of the key is the responsibility of the nursing staff. It should never be given to a patient. If there are no mixer taps, the key will turn on the hot water tap.

Always run the bath for the patient. Fill it so that the patient's thighs are immersed and check the temperature. (A bath thermometer should be used for this purpose.) The water should be 38°C. *Where there are no mixer taps, run the cold water in first.*

Requirements
    Change of clothing for the patient
    Soap and face cloth
    Talcum powder, deodorants, etc.
    Bath towel and hand towel
    Bath mat
    Chair.

Method
Whether the patient has fetched his own things or whether you have done so, make sure everything required is at hand. Once the bathing begins you should not leave the patient unsupervised.

Like all nursing activities, this may well be a teaching situation for the patient and you should encourage him to do as much for himself as possible. After the patient is undressed he is helped into the bath. Always supervise this. Many handicapped persons have poor muscular coordination and although they appear quite competent when standing on both feet, or when walking, they may be quite unable to keep their balance when climbing into the bath. If the patient is helpless he will need to be lifted into the bath from a chair or trolley. Two or more nurses may be required for this.

Bathing should be done briskly and quickly. Let the patient help if he is able. Encourage him to follow the routine of soaping his face cloth, washing, and then rinsing the parts of his body. Inspect the patient's

body for abnormalities while you are working. Try to avoid frivolities. Handicapped patients are easily excited and can then become quite unmanageable. After the bathing dry the patient thoroughly, paying particular attention to the skin folds, e.g. the armpits, under the breasts, the groins, and between the toes. Apply talcum power, deodorants, etc. Let the patient help if possible. Try to establish a routine so that the patient systematically dries one area of the body and then moves to the next. This is followed by dressing. Afterwards the bathroom is tidied up, the bath disinfected and made ready for the next patient.

Special points
The supply of towels and face cloths varies with different hospitals. Some hospitals allow the patients to have their own towels and face cloths, and in that case they will be brought into the bathroom and taken away when the patient is finished. In other hospitals a supply of clean towels and face cloths is kept in the bathroom, and discarded into the used linen container after each patient has been bathed. Disposable face cloths are also used in some hospital wards. Whichever method is adopted, each

patient must be given a towel and face cloth for his own use; the same towels and face cloths should never be used for several patients.

The difficult patient
1 Do not lock or bolt the door while you are working so that other people can get in if you need help.
2 Make sure that you have the bath-tap key on your person.
3 If a patient becomes difficult to manage, pull out the bath plug and call for help. In most cases this is all that is required and you can then proceed with drying.

Bedbathing
This procedure is adopted for patients who are not able to be taken to the bathroom. As these patients are usually helpless, two nurses should work together.

Requirements
A bathing trolley with:

Two bathing sheets
Large jug with hot water
Basin
Pail for used water
Soap, face cloths, nailbrush
Bath towel and face towel
Talcum powder
Brush and comb
Clean bed linen and nightgown
Materials used for treatment of pressure areas
Nail scissors
Disposal bag
Linen bags on carriers for soiled and foul linen.

Method
Take all the requirements to the bedside, screen the bed and close the nearby windows.
   Place clean nightgown or pyjamas onto a suitable radiator to warm. Pour the water into the basin on the trolley. Remove the top bedclothes, except for one blanket. Roll one bathing sheet under the patient. Place the second bathing sheet on top of the patient. Remove the blanket from underneath the sheet. Undress the patient. Pass the face towel to the second nurse and wash the patient's face. Rinse the face cloth while the other nurse dries the face. Then lay the face cloth and face towel aside

n the trolley. Hand the other nurse the bath towel. Using the second
ace cloth, proceed to wash the patient's hands and arms, chest, and
bdomen, washing, rinsing and drying the parts as you go along. Change
he water as required. Turn the patient onto his side to wash the back
nd the pubic area. Always change the water after this is done. Wash
nd dry the legs and feet. Cover each area once it is finished to avoid
nnecessary exposure of the patient. Add more hot water to the basin if
he water in it gets cold.

The patient's pressure areas may be treated as you proceed with
athing, or you may undertake this task after the bathing is finished.
'alcum powder should be applied sparingly on the body, especially in
hose places where two skin surfaces touch. Inspect the finger and toe
ails. Brush and cut, if necessary. Remove the bathing sheets, dress the
atient and make up the bed. Tidy the hair so that the patient is
omfortable. Remove the equipment, draw the screens back and tidy up.

Special points

Patients who are bathed in bed are usually very helpless. Be gentle and careful when moving the patient. If necessary, get extra help for turning the patient so that he is not dragged about the bed. Talk to the patient while you are working. He may not take part in the conversation, but he should hear a gentle and reassuring voice while you are with him.

While bathing, exercise the patient's limbs and put the joints through the range of movements of which they are capable. Do this gently and systematically, including shoulder, elbow, wrist, fingers, hip, knee and ankle joints, and move the toes. This may be the only exercise that the patient gets, if he is not able to move at all.

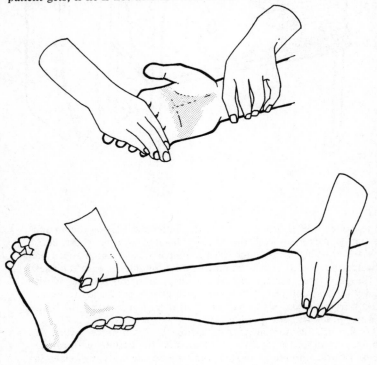

If the bed has cot sides, never leave the cot side down, unless you are standing beside the bed. If you turn away even for a few moments, put the cot side up.

Care of Pressure Areas

Pressure areas is the term applied to parts of the body where the skin may be damaged because of excessive pessure, friction, or continued exposure to moisture. A healthy person is able to change his position frequently to avoid excessive pressure on any one part of the body; he is quickly aware of the burning sensation on the skin if he is exposed to friction, and he is able to keep his body clean and dry. Many handicapped patients are not able to do these things so the nurse must constantly be aware of the fact that her patients may damage their skin. The nurse who observes her patients closely will be able to anticipate trouble and act accordingly.

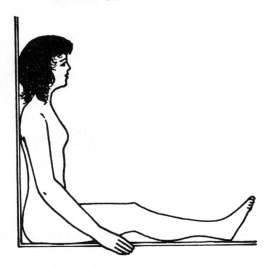

Patients at risk

All patients who cannot readily move all, or parts of their bodies are at risk of lying too long in one position. This impairs the blood supply to those parts of the body and the skin will redden and break. In these patients the following precautions must be taken:

1 The patient's position should be changed every two hours, day and night.
2 The skin should be massaged to stimulate the circulation.
3 The body should be placed in such a way that limbs do not press on each other.

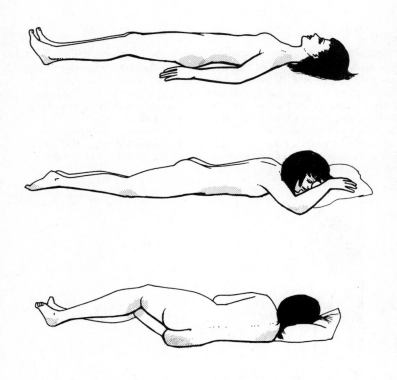

4 Air cushions, pressure pads and airbeds should be used when required.

All patients who are incontinent of urine or faeces, or both, whether they are confined to bed or not, are liable to excoriation of the skin if the parts of the body that become wet and soiled are not washed and dried. All patients who perspire profusely are also at risk where perspiration is trapped between skin surfaces, e.g. in axilla and groin or, in obese female patients, under the breasts. All those who dribble saliva onto the chin and neck are also at risk. Precautions to be taken are:

1 Patients must be attended to whenever they are wet or soiled.
2 The affected parts of the body must be washed thoroughly and then dried. Wiping the skin dry of perspiration, saliva or urine without washing is not sufficient.

Position	Position of Feet	Time	Mon	Tue	Wed	Thur	Fri	Sat	Sun
LEFT LATERAL		4 AM	*QR*						
		NOON	*AJ*						
		20.00 HRS	*W*						
DORSAL		6 AM	*QR*						
		14.00 HRS	*W*						
		22.00 HRS	*QR*						
RIGHT LATERAL		8 AM	*AJ*						
		16.00 HRS	*W*						
		24.00 HRS	*QR*						
PRONE		10 AM	*AJ*						
		18.00 HRS	*W*						
		2 AM	*QR*						

3 Barrier creams may be applied to give some protection after the skin has been washed and dried. It does not take the place of washing, nor does it do away with the need to attend to the patient whenever he is wet.
4 Protective plastic pants, bedsheets, etc. will be used to protect the patient's clothing, but again it must be remembered that these do not protect the skin.

All patients who are hyperactive, or who perform repetitive movements with parts of their bodies are liable to pressure sores in these areas. This applies to restless patients who are confined to bed, those lying on playmats or sitting in chairs, as well as those who are up and about. Patients who have a peculiar gait may have their feet damaged because their shoes do not yield to their particular requirements. Similarly, in patients whose way of walking is awkward, skin in the groin may become damaged by rubbing against clothing. Elbows or parts of the head may be affected because of friction caused by persistent movement. In all these patients the skin must be inspected at least once daily and protected.

Precautions

1   Unsuitable footwear should be reported so that orthopaedic adjustments may be made. Exercises may be ordered to correct bad walking habits, and these will require to be supervised by the nurses.
2   Protective pads may be applied to parts of the body where friction is reddening the skin.
3   If the patient is performing repetitive movements which are damaging his skin then his attention should be distracted and his activities directed elsewhere.

Diabetic patients

Special care must be taken with all diabetic patients. Their skin should be inspected at bath time and any reddened or broken areas of skin treated immediately. Nails must be cut with care. Special attention must be paid to the fitting of shoes; if necessary, special shoes must be made to ensure that the feet are not injured by wearing ill-fitting footwear.

Routine care of pressure areas

Requirements

Water in basin, soap and towel
Methylated spirit, if that is the policy of the ward
Talcum powder
Barrier cream, e.g. silicone cream
Nourishing cream, e.g. cod liver oil cream
Tissues, or brown wool, to remove excreta
Plastic sheets, plastic pants, incontinence pads to protect bedding and clothing
Disposal bag for soiled articles
Clean linen
Carriers with bags for soiled and foul linen.

Method

Take the requirements to the patient and screen the bed, or take the patient to the bathroom. Renove the soiled and wet clothing. Use tissues or brown wool to clean the patient. Then wash the area with soap and water and, with a soapy hand, massage the skin in a circular movement to stimulate the circulation. If allowed and indicated, then after drying, the skin is rubbed with methylated spirit. This must never be done on skin which is already broken. Spirit may be useful in cases where friction is responsible for potential skin damage. After drying, the skin may be dusted with talcum powder to make it smooth. If moisture is likely to damage the skin, a barrier cream should be applied. A nourishing cream may be a useful alternative. Whatever is used, it should be applied sparingly and smoothed into the skin. Afterwards the bed is made, or the patient dressed, whichever applies.

Tidy up and wash the patient's hands. Any extra appliances used, as for instance pressure pads or air mattresses, should be firmly in place.

Ripple beds for the helpless bedridden patient have proved useful. An

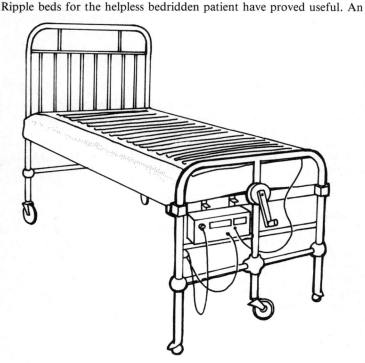

airbed is placed on the mattress and air is pumped into alternate sections of the bed by means of an electric pump. This helps to distribute the patient's weight over different parts of the body. If a ripple bed is in use, the patient may be turned every four hours instead of every two, but the need to attend to the patient's skin in every other way still applies. Make sure that the tubing leading to the mattress is not obstructed and that the bed is inflated to the right pressure. The patient's weight should not compress the air mattress completely, nor should the bed be blown up to such a pressure that it becomes hard and unyielding.

Pressure sore
A *pressure sore* is the term applied to a pressure area where, despite all precautions, the skin has broken and there is an open sore. This may be small and superficial involving skin only, or it may be a deep hole exposing muscle and even bone.

Every pressure sore, however small, should be reported to the person in charge, and should then be treated. There is no standard treatment and whatever has been ordered will have to be applied. Remember that pressure sores are open wounds and require to be treated by sterile techniques.

Moving and Lifting Patients

Moving and lifting of helpless patients requires skill so that the patient is not subject to unnecessary discomfort and the nurse is not exposed to undue exertion with resulting backstrain.

A selection of mechanical lifting aids is available for use in a person's own home as well as in hospitals and other institutions. Personnel require instruction in how to use them efficiently, and the mentally handicapped person needs to become accustomed to apparatus such as a hoist.

Ambulation
Help and support from the nurse will be required by the patient when he gets up out of bed for the first time. This can apply to the patient who has been confined to bed for a short time following surgery or to the patient who has been confined to bed for a considerable time.

The patient who is getting out of bed for the first time following surgery is more likely to suffer pain and discomfort when he gets up.

The patient who is getting up out of bed after being confined to bed for a considerable time usually has weak muscles due to lack of use although exercises and physiotherapy while he has been bedbound can help to reduce the effect of prolonged bed rest.

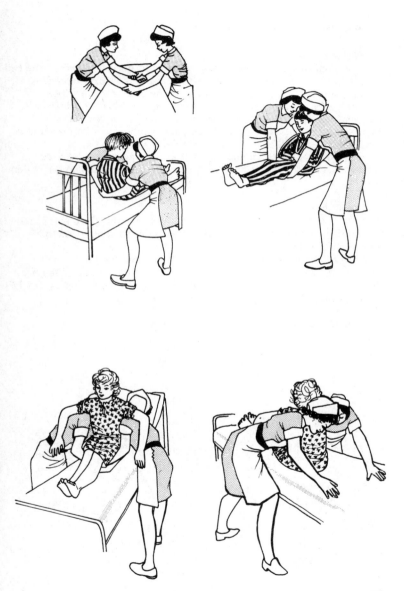

Getting the patient out of bed

Preparing the chair
It is essential that the patient is kept warm and out of draughts. The bed should be screened and windows and doors in the vicinity closed. A dressing gown, socks, and slippers will be required for the patient.
A suitable chair should be at the bedside and this may be draped with a blanket. The type of chair will depend on the patient's condition. For example an elderly or debilitated patient should not be placed in a low chair which will be difficult to rise from when the patient is returning to bed. The chair used should be comfortable and give good back support. There should be no pressure behind the knees when the patient is sitting.

Preparing the patient
The top bed clothes should be removed. The dressing gown and socks put on. Two or more nurses should be available to support the patient who should be helped into the sitting position in bed.
  While one nurse supports the patient (sometimes two nurses are needed) the other nurse lifts the patient's legs over the side of the bed. Slippers should be put on at this point. The soles of the slippers should be non-slippery.

One nurse assisting patient from bed to chair

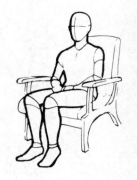

If the bed is too high a footstool on a firm base can usually help the patient when he is stepping out of bed.

The patient is sat down in a prepared chair at the bedside. The feet are put on a footstool if desired and the blankets tucked round him for warmth. The nurse should ask if he is comfortable and move any articles he may need within reach—spectacles, newspaper, tissues, drinking glass and so on.

Two nurses assisting patient from bed to chair

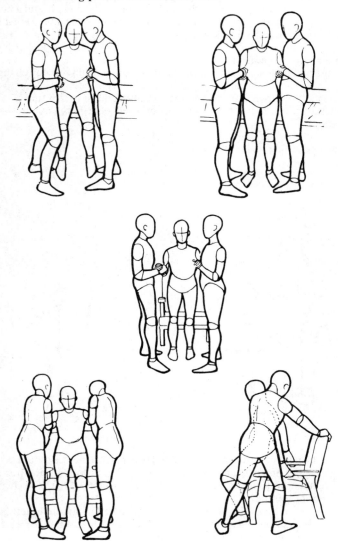

Preparing the bed for the patient's return
When the patient is out of bed it should be stripped and remade and a hot water bottle put in it in preparation for his return. A warm bed is a great joy when the paient returns a little weary.

Observation of the patient
When the patient is sitting up the nurse should observe him for any changes in his condition. If there are any these should be reported.

There are usually specific instructions regarding the length of time a patient may be up. It may be for a very short spell—five or ten minutes—the first time.

One nurse assisting patient to stand

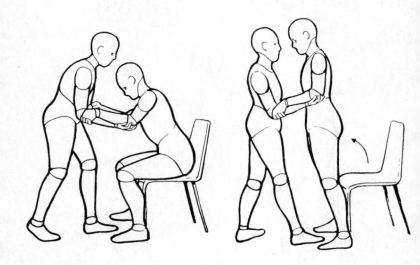

When the patient is due to return to bed two or more nurses should be available to give him help and support. The use of the footstool as a step to help the patient to climb into bed is helpful—particularly if the bed is high and cannot be lowered.

When the patient has been returned to bed he should be left in a comfortable position and allowed to rest. Again the nurse should observe her patient for any change in his condition.

Two nurses assisting patient back to bed

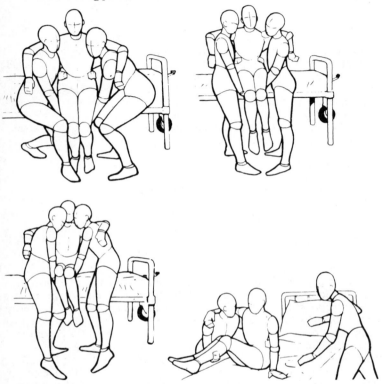

Patients sometimes feel faint and dizzy when they are getting up for the first time. This usually passes when the sitting position is reached. Patients who have been up to sit for several periods gradually increase their activities. Nurses give support when the patient begins to walk.

Some patients need to be retaught to walk by the physiotherapist but the nurse will continue this treatment in the absence of the physiotherapist. It is therefore most important that the nurse should see how the physiotherapist tackles this problem.

It is very important that the patients do not overtire themselves when they begin to walk again. Remember to warn them if they are over zealous that they have to walk back the distance they have covered from base!

Facial Appearance

Shaving: male patients

As the mentally handicapped male grows up he will usually require to shave. If the young man is in a hospital, lives in a hostel, or attends a day training centre, the staff should make it their responsibility to include shaving in the daily routine. This means that the person's ability must be assessed to see how far he can learn to perform this task himself, and which method of shaving is best suited to his needs. It is very important to develop right attitudes by getting him to accept that having a clean-shaven face is part of good grooming and is as important as being clean and tidy. Moustaches and beards also require grooming.

Wet shaving requirements
   Shaving brush
   Safety razor and blades (or disposable razor)
   Shaving soap or cream
   Wash-hand basin with good light and mirror
   Towel
   Receptacle for used razor blades.

Procedure

Collect, or get the patient to collect the requirements and take them to the basin. Insist that the patient takes off his shirt or turns down the collar to prevent it getting wet. Then show the patient how to load the brush with soap, and lather the face and neck including only those parts which have to be shaved. It may take some time to teach the patient to do just that for himself, and during the early part of the training programme the nurse might well have to do the actual shaving herself until the patient is able to master the first part. Encourage the patient to watch the shaving process in the mirror, so that he can see what is being done time and time again. This gives him a chance to remember the routine for when he is able to do it. Discipline yourself always to proceed in the same order, shaving one part of the face first, followed by others, and tell him what you are doing. Encourage him to try each time to do the shaving himself, and he will gradually learn how to hold the razor and shave the easier parts of his face himself. Let him wash and dry his face when the shaving is done, and get him to tidy up with you afterwards. Whether the patient is allowed to handle the razor blade or not will depend on the personality of the patient as well as on his manual dexterity, and with some patients a disposable razor complete with sealed blade is preferable. In any case, always supervise the patient and do not leave him alone.

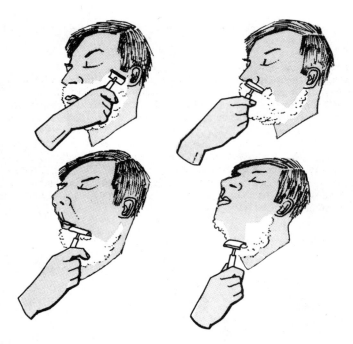

Dry shaving

This is done with an electric razor. The patient may have his own razor, but much more commonly the ward or hostel has a wall-mounted fitting near a mirror from which a heavy-duty electric razor can be worked. It is usually easier for the patient to learn to use an electric razor and there is less danger that he will cut himself. Some patients will be encouraged by the fascination of the electric gadget to include shaving in their daily routine and, if this is so, then this method should be preferred to a safety razor. After-shave creams or lotions can be used if they are available and if the patient can be persuaded to spend some of his pocket money to buy these things. It may, however, be necessary to provide some face cream for certain patients whose skin is flaky and dry.

Sometimes older patients are admitted to hospital who have not previously established a shaving habit. In these patients the nurse will have to persevere until the patient accepts this as part of his daily routine. It may well be necessary, if the patient will not try to learn to shave, to delay his breakfast until he has made a reasonable attempt.

Not all patients can learn how to shave themselves, and in any hospital for the handicapped there will be large numbers of patients who will have to be shaved by the staff.

Shaving: female patients
Among the mentally handicapped there are quite a number of female patients who have a strong growth of facial hair. This can be embarrassing to the sensitive patient and her relatives and visitors and lead to her being unduly shy and withdrawn. In these cases the facial hair should be removed.

When the hairs on the face are few, it may be possible to teach the patient the use of tweezers to pull out the hairs periodically, or the nurse can do this for her. Each hair should be removed individually, the line of pull with the tweezers being in the natural direction of the hair's growth to make sure that the hair is removed and not broken. Epilation has to be repeated when the hair grows again.

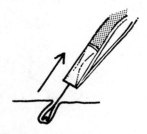

When facial growth is thick as on the male, shaving is indicated and should be taught to the patient. The use of an electric razor is appropriate and generally meets the needs of the patient.

Underarm hair may be unsightly, and although the same shaving procedures apply it is much more difficult for the female to shave this area herself without inflicting injury. The nurse should always assist in this. She should also supervise the procedure when hair removing creams are applied as they can damage the skin when left on too long.

Make-up
Many handicapped girls take an interest in the application of make-up, and the nurse can instruct the patients in its correct use. Small groups of patients can be given beauty care classes where they learn how to make the best of their appearance. The nurse can recommend preparations which are suitable for her patients and introduce them to beauty aids which they might not get to know otherwise, such as creams which hide blemishes. It is a good idea to make certain that the hospital shop stocks

those preparations which are recommended, so that the patients can safely spend some of their pocket money on these products.

It is to be remembered, however, that in spite of every encouragement some patients remain uninterested in their appearance. In that case it is the nurse's function to do for the patient what she will not do for herself.

Care of the Hair

Carefully groomed hair which is clean enhances the appearance and gives a feeling of confidence. For the mentally handicapped patient this is of great importance as she may be endowed with detracting physical features which cannot be hidden and then an attractive modern hairstyle will do much to divert the onlooker's attention.

Care of the hair includes:

1 Inspecting and treating for dandruff and headlice
2 Brushing and combing
3 Cutting and styling
4 Washing and setting
5 Permanent waving and tinting.

Inspection of the hair

Hair should be inspected routinely once a week to make sure that all patients are free from dandruff, headlice, scratchmarks on the scalp, etc. It should also be examined when newly admitted and when patients return from leave.

Requirements
    Gown for the nurse
    Plastic cape
    Dressing comb
    Fine toothed comb
    Packet of cotton wool balls
    Disposal bag.

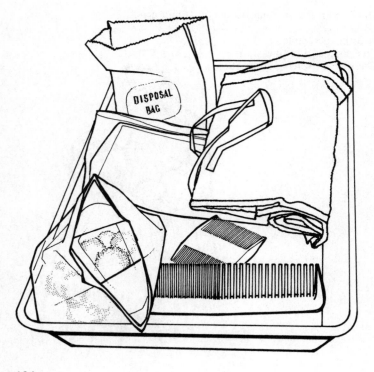

Method

For the patient who is up and about, this is best done in the bathroom; for the bedbound patient, screens are required to ensure privacy. The nurse will explain to the patient what is to be done, and will then put on the gown. After the cape has been placed round the patient's shoulders, the nurse carefully and gently combs the hair with the dressing comb so that it is free from tangles. The hair is then parted into small sections which are combed with the fine toothed comb. A cotton wool ball held behind the comb should be inspected each time for the presence of lice, and discarded into the disposal bag. After the whole head has been inspected the hair is combed into the usual style unless it requires to be treated.

Head lice

Head lice are pale grey in colour and about one millimetre in length. They are most frequently seen in the area behind and above the ears, and can also occur on the eyebrows and eyelashes. Their movement on the scalp causes itching, and scratchmarks are common on the scalps of affected patients. If present in large numbers, they are not difficult to detect, but careful inspection is necessary to avoid missing small numbers, especially when dandruff is also present.

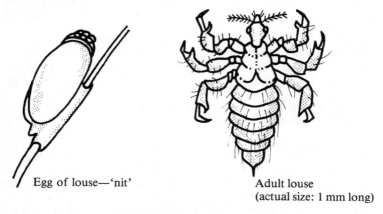

Egg of louse—'nit'

Adult louse
(actual size: 1 mm long)

The eggs of lice are called nits. They can be found firmly attached to the hairshafts close to the hair roots. Before hatching, which takes place about four days after they are laid, they appear as small transparent white round specks about the size of a small pinhead. After hatching the egg case remains attached to the hair as a tiny light grey flake.

Treatment of infested hair
This is undertaken immediately after detection to avoid spread.

Requirements
In addition to the articles needed for inspection, the following should be provided:

1 Bowl with disinfectant for the cotton wool balls containing vermin
2 Lotion or cream recommended for treatment
3 Gallipot for lotion.

Method
This will depend on the preparation used. It is important that the manufacturer's instructions are followed so that success is ensured.

Nits should be removed from the hair by using a vinegar solution (5%) or nit removing fluid. After the solution has loosened the nits from the hair shafts, they can be pulled off by passing cotton wool down the strands of hair.

After treatment the hair should be combed into the usual style.

Aftercare
Infested hair should be inspected daily and treatment repeated, should this be necessary, until all traces of lice have been removed. Afterwards the hair should be washed.

Treatment for dandruff
Dandruff should be treated by washing the hair with a special shampoo. Several different brands are on the market, and more than one brand may have to be tried before success is achieved. Preparations containing *selenium sulphide* are best for this purpose, but they should not be used too frequently lest they irritate the scalp.

Brushing and combing
Hair should be brushed morning and evening, and combed when tousled. Each patient should have her own brush and comb and should be encouraged to take an interest in her appearance. Teaching the patient to do her own hair is best done in front of a mirror so that results can be seen. Gentleness on the part of the nurse is needed when disentangling tousled hair so that the patient is not hurt, and as a result of this discouraged from taking an interest in this activity.

Pocket combs which can be carried about may be provided, or the patients may spend some of their pocket money on buying these if it encourages them to keep their hair tidy.

Helpless patients will have their hair arranged by the nurse in a style which is attractive and comfortable.

Cutting and styling
This is on the whole a task for the expert and should be done by professional hairdressers. If the hospital has its own hairdressing department appointments for cutting will be made for the patients by the nurses, or the patients may make their own appointments if they are fit to do so. The nurse should help in choosing a style which is suitable for the patient, bearing in mind that hair style fashions change, and that, while the extremes of high fashion may not be desirable, patients will not wish to wear styles that are obviously outmoded. It must also be borne in mind that the parents of children and young adults should be consulted when a drastic change in style is contemplated.

Washing and setting
Helpless patients will have to have their hair washed in bed.

Once the patient is comfortably settled and well supported the hair can be washed. If the patient is nervous a small amount of warm water should be poured over his head till he gets used to it. The nurse then wets the hair thoroughly and applies an adequate amount of shampoo which is gently massaged into the scalp. This is a very comfortable and pleasant thing to have done so do not hurry the procedure.

The hair is then rinsed either by pouring water from a small jug, or water squeezed from a water-loaded sponge against the head to expel the water. The method of rinsing is repeated until the hair is thoroughly rinsed. Remember that 'clean hair squeaks'!

At this point the head is wrapped in a warm towel and all washing equipment removed.

Drying hair

Gently but quickly the patient's hair is partially dried by mopping and rubbing. Any clothes or bedclothes which have become damp are changed. The patient is settled comfortably in bed. The hair is then combed and arranged in a practical, suitable, and attractive style. It can then be completely dried with a hair dryer.

Hairdressing facilities for the patients who are up and about in a hospital or hostel for the mentally handicapped will rarely be adequate to cope with a weekly 'wash and set' and the nurses will have to do this for the patients on the ward. Many patients can be taught to do at least the washing of the hair

for themselves, and providing the female wards have hairdriers and
equipment such as rollers for setting the hair, the opportunity is there for
the nurse not only to teach her patients the way to wash the hair but also to
influence their taste and their attitudes toward a well-groomed appearance.

Permanent waving and tinting
This should be done by professional hairdressers who will apply the correct
choice of treatment which suits the hair texture of the individual. 'Colour

rinses' may be applied on the ward as a special treat when a patient goes to a party or on a special outing.

Curly or frizzy hair
Very curly or frizzy hair can sometimes be a problem if it is neglected or infested. Some of the proprietary fluids to straighten hair can be used during the period of cleaning such hair.

When treatment stops the fluid can be stopped and the hair will then grow curly or frizzy again.

Care of Ears, Eyes, Nose and Mouth

Care of ears
Inspection of the ears is necessary at regular intervals to see that they are clean. If the patient is helpless and the nurse attends to bathing and washing, then the ears will be inspected and cleaned during bathtime. However, many patients who are quite capable of washing themselves and who require only a minimum of supervision when bathing are unwilling or unable to wash their ears, and inspection is therefore needed. At the same time the nurse should check up to see that there is no discharge from the ears. Excess wax can be removed by using cotton wool on the end of an organge stick, but the stick must not be pushed into the ear lest it damage the ear drum. The ears of babies and small children should be carefully cleaned in the same way.

Discharging ears must be reported to the medical staff who will order treatment, if necessary.

Care of the eyes
Eyes should be inspected after the morning wash to see that lids are free from crusts. If necessary, they should be wiped with cotton wool, using warm water or saline. They should be wiped from the nasal side outwards, using a fresh piece of wool every time. Inflammation of the lids occurs in multiple sclerosis patients especially and also in some patients who have a habit of rubbing their eyes. Discharge from the eyes is a sign of infection and must be reported so that it can be treated. It may be necessary to isolate a patient with an eye infection to prevent the spread of the infection.

Care of the nose
In babies, small children and helpless patients it will be necessary to clean the nose with cotton wool on the end of an orange stick. For older children and adults paper tissues should be used to keep the nose free from discharge. It is part of the nursing care of handicapped patients to

teach them as far as possible how to use and dispose of paper tissues. Washable handkerchiefs may be used, but they are easily lost, or misused. Colds and chronic or purulent nasal discharges should be reported. Many patients are susceptible to colds and may develop respiratory complications; as far as possible, patients with colds should be separated from the others.

Care of the teeth and mouth
Daily care of the teeth and mouth is an essential part of nursing care for all handicapped patients. As with skin care, the routine adopted will vary with the degree of ability of the patient.

Routine brushings of teeth
All those who are capable of learning how to care for their teeth should be taught to do so. Persistent and patient effort on the part of the nursing staff can help a large number of patients to follow the routine of cleaning their teeth first thing in the morning and last thing at night. It is good practice to attend to the cleaning of teeth when face and hands are washed in the morning and at night.

Requirements
    Toothbrush labelled with the patient's own name
    Toothpaste or dentrifice
    Toothmug
    Towel at the wash hand basin.

It is advisable to have only one patient at a time at each wash-hand basin so that he can concentrate fully on the task in hand and is not distracted. The tasks that each patient will have to master are:

1 Applying the toothpaste or dentrifice to the brush
2 Brushing the teeth up and down
3 Rinsing of the mouth and spitting out the water into the basin
4 Rinsing the toothbrush.

Sometimes it is not possible to teach the patient how to apply the toothpaste to the brush, and in cases where wastage is high because the patient finds this task, which requires a certain degree of fine muscle coordination, too difficult it may be possible to teach him to use dentrifice or, as an alternative, the nurse should prepare the toothbrush for him. At the end of the procedure the patient should be taught to rinse his brush and mug, and return these to the place of storage.

Storage of toothbrushes can often be a problem. If the patients in the ward do not use sponge-bags, there may be racks in the vicinity of the wash-hand basins on which the brushes are placed. Each place in the rack is labelled with a patient's name or a picture, and, providing he can identify his own place, he will return the brush to the right place on the rack. When only small numbers of patients who cannot read at all are involved, then it is possible to use symbols or pictures for identification. The return of toothbrushes to racks should always be supervised by the nurse to make sure that brushes are not mixed up. In some wards the brushes are immersed in a mild disinfectant. Disposable toothbrushes may be used.

The care of the gums is particularly important in epileptic patients who are on drugs, as some of these may cause excessive growth of the gums.

Care of the mouth and teeth of helpless patients
Severely handicapped patients, and all those who are confined to bed, will not be able to care for their teeth and the nurse will have to do this.

Requirements
A tray set with the following:

3 gallipots
Packet of swabs and cotton wool
Orange sticks
2 pairs of artery or dressing forceps
1 bottle of glycothymoline, 5% solution
1 bottle of sodium bicarbonate, 5% solution
1 bottle of glycerine and lemon
Wooden spatula and mouthgag (optional)
1 disposal bag
1 dressing cape, or disposable towel.

Procedure
Draw the screens round the bed and place the tray so that you can reach it easily when standing beside the patient. Make the patient comfortable so that you have access to his mouth without having to turn his head.

Pour some of the lotions from the bottles into the gallipots. You need only a few drops of glycerine and lemon for each ptient. Open the packet containing the swabs and cotton wool and load a few orange sticks by wrapping some cotton wool round each end of the stick. (Note: in some wards you will get packets of orange sticks with cotton wool already prepared and sterilised for use.) Place the cape or towel round the patient's neck to protect the bedclothes and proceed as follows. Using orange sticks for the teeth and forceps with swabs for the mouth, dip in sodium bicarbonate solution, clean the teeth, the inside of the cheeks and tongue and remove all traces of food. Follow this by using

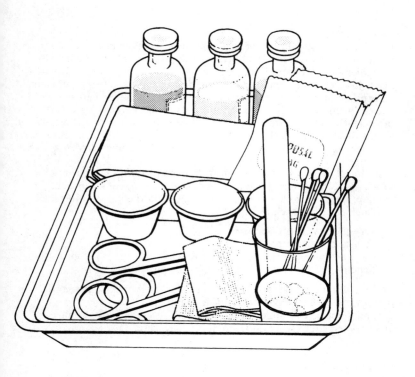

glycothymoline in the same manner, leaving the mouth clean and fresh. If the tongue and lips are dry, apply a little glycerine and lemon. Use each orange stick or swab only once and dispose of it into the paper bag. A wooden spatula may be needed to help clean the tongue. In patients who are completely unable to cooperate you may require a mouthgag to keep the mouth open. When finished, clear away the equipment and clean the tray, topping it up ready for use again. Wash your hands.

Special Points
Always work gently and take care not to induce retching and vomiting when cleaning the back of the tongue.

If the mouth is very dirty and coated with dry material, you may use hydrogen peroxide solution, 10%, instead of sodium bicarbonate. Its foaming action helps to loosen any sordes (crusts) but it can taste unpleasant to the patient and he may vomit.

113

Care of artificial dentures

Denture plates should be marked with the patient's name to avoid their being lost or mislaid and each patient should also have a labelled container for his dentures into which they are placed at night. He also needs his own brush and cleaning solution or tablets. The denture should be brushed at night either by the patient or by the nurse before it is placed in the container. If several patients in the ward have dentures, take great care not to mix them up. Always clean them one at a time and return them to the labelled containers immediately. Store the containers overnight in a secure place where they cannot be tampered with by other patients.

Artificial dentures must fit well if they are to fulfil their purpose. When the gums change with increasing age the original set of dentures may no longer fit well and the patient may find them uncomfortable.

Watch for signs such as:

Refusal to wear the dentures
Refusal of certain foods
Sores on tongue or gums and bleeding
Slackness of the teeth when the patient speaks.

In these instances your observations should be reported and recorded so that arrangements can be made for a dental appointment.

It may not be advisable for patients with severe epilepsy to have dentures lest they choke on them during a seizure.

Observations on the mouth and teeth

The healthy mouth is kept moist by the flow of saliva from the salivary glands. The saliva is swallowed. There is a continuous secretion of saliva which is increased in health at the sight, smell, or thought of food and when food is eaten.

This normal pattern may be upset temporarily through illness, or permanently by any disability which is associated with difficulty in swallowing. Temporary illness accompanied by a rise in temperature, reduction in appetite, and dehydration produces a dry mouth. The nurse must watch for this, and the resulting halitosis, cracked lips, and the appearance of sordes in the mouth which lead to further loss of appetite, nausea, ulceration of the mouth, and the possibility of the inhalation of dry particles present. Cleaning of the mouth should under these circumstances be carried out every 4 hours. A white curd-like deposit can sometimes be observed in the mouths of babies, or debilitated children and adults. This may be an infection called *thrush*, and should always be reported.

Mouth breathing is a common problem in handicapped patients. This leads to dryness of the mouth which should be watched for and counteracted by frequent cleaning and adequate fluid intake. Patients should be encouraged to keep their mouths shut and breathe through the nose.

Excessive salivation and/or the inability to swallow saliva is also found in a large number of handicapped people. It is associated with patients who have difficulty in swallowing and may be a side effect of some drugs, e.g. phenothiazines. Atropine-like drugs can be used to reduce excessive salivation. In the helpless bedridden patient dribbling saliva can lead to skin rashes on face and neck due to constant wetness, and for this, protective cream may be used after careful washing and drying of the skin.

Other abnormalities that the nurse should look for are the presence of dental decay, badly crowded teeth, absence of teeth, badly fitting dentures and coating of the tongue.

Care of the Nails

To ensure the comfort of the patient and also to improve his appearance hands, feet and nails should be carefully attended to. This involves not only the cutting of the nails but also the correct choice of shoes, socks and stockings.

Cutting of fingernails
Requirements:
    Pair of nail scissors
    Disposable towel
    Disposal bag.

Fingernails should be cut weekly. In some instances it may be advisable to cut them more frequently, as for example in young children who scratch themselves, and then the careful trimming of nails every other day may avoid the use of mittens to prevent them scratching themselves, or other children. Cut the nails short, shaping them slightly at the corners. Examine the fingers to see if the cuticles have ragged edges. The skin of the hands should be smooth and soft and should not show any roughness. If skin is roughened cream should be applied at night and a check should be made on the kind of soap used, as the kind of soap used for hand washing may account for the roughness of the hands. If disposable hand towels are used it is worthwhile checking if they are soft and absorbent enough to dry the hands quickly. Hard paper towels which do not dry easily may well be the cause of rough hands.

Manicuring of nails
Handicapped female patients can be encouraged to take pride in their appearance by teaching them to care for their nails under supervision. They can be taught how to use a nail-file and how, by growing them slightly longer, to shape their nails. Nail polish and polish remover may be provided, or bought by the patients with their own pocket money. They can be helped to apply this. They can be encouraged to file them and apply polish when they prepare themselves for going to parties or on outings.

Applying polish to the nails involves delicate movements and helps a patient to practice hand-eye coordination, while at the same time showing her an immediate result for her patience and effort. Removal of the polish tidily and completely can be a pre-condition to further use of nail polish and can give the patient experience in using a liquid in an economical way. It also offers one of the few opportunities for allowing a patient to practice the use of both hands in a situation where she has an incentive to persevere.

Cutting of toenails
Requirements:
  Pair of sharp, strong, curved nail scissors
  Pair of nail clippers
  Disposable towel
  Disposal bag.

The feet should be clean and dry. It is often suitable to do this after the patient has had a bath. Inspect the feet and then proceed to cut the nails short and straight across, using either the scissors or the clippers if the nails are strong. Collect the clippings on the towel and place them in the disposal bag. Take care not to hurt the patient by forcing the scissors under the nail.

Toenails can be cut once a week. Bath time is best when the nails are softer from immersion in water. The nurse records her observation on the condition of the patient's feet in the nurse's notes, or in a book which may be kept for this purpose. Information recorded should include the inability to cut a patient's nails, any in-growing nails, corns, the presence of hard skin and any other abnormalities which require the referral of the patient to the care of the chiropodist.

In large wards where there are many patients it is sometimes the routine to cut all the patients' nails at bedtime so that no one is missed.

16

Toilet Training and Sexual Functions

Training handicapped patients to gain bladder and bowel control is one of the very important aspects of nursing care. Normal children can be expected to have control around the age of two years. Handicapped people are much slower in this respect and a proportion of severely handicapped patients will remain incontinent all their lives.

Training should be started when a patient begins to take an interest in his surroundings and when he begins to demand attention. It should also be attempted in all patients who are admitted to hospital irrespective of age, where training at home has not been successful.

A training programme should be prepared for the patient and all nurses should be required to participate so that continuity of training is assured. The training programme must also be continued at school or occupation centre and, if possible, the cooperation of parents and relatives should be sought so that training is not interrupted when the patient leaves hospital for weekends or holidays.

It is important that the nurse gets to know the signs which indicate that a patient requires to be taken to the toilet. Ideally the patient will express his needs verbally, but often this is not possible, and the nurse will have to watch for the changes in the patient's behaviour which precede the emptying of the bladder. Fidgeting, loss of concentration on the task in hand, interruption of play for no apparent reason are some of the signs that indicate toilet needs.

Definite times should be laid down when patients use 'pots' or are taken to the toilet to empty their bladders. These times are usually related to rising in the morning, to mealtimes and playtimes, before going out of the ward, and bedtimes. Individual adjustments may have to be made according to the patient's bladder capacity. A fairly constant fluid intake at certain times of the day helps a little in anticipating the patients' needs and reduces the risks of 'accidents' especially in those patients who are in the process of achieving some success, and who can be discouraged by the occasional failure.

It is essential to make sure that the patients are comfortably warm in the ward at times when they are not physically active, as coldness increases the frequency with which the bladder empties.

Bowel training is best undertaken immediately after breakfast, since this is the time of day when the bowel is most likely to open. While allowing an adequate amount of time for the patient to empty the bowel, he should not be asked to sit in the toilet too long lest the reason for being there is forgotten. Some people do not normally have a bowel motion every day and it may not be realistic to expect the bowel to open every day, especially if the person is on a diet low in roughage.

Some patients may have constipation which cannot be corrected by dietary measures. If suppositories or enemas are ordered to correct constipation, their administration should be related to the habit training programme and administration should be before the patient would be taken to the toilet after breakfast.

The routine of hand-washing after visits to the toilet should be introduced at the same time so that this habit is linked to toilet training from the very outset.

As in other training situations it is important that praise is given and that scolding is avoided. The patient should receive constant encouragement when success is achieved. Operant conditioning may be helpful in establishing bladder and bowel control.

Menstruation
The first day of each menstrual period should be noted and a written record kept of the menstrual cycle of the patients. During the periods the patient will have to be supervised if necessary and supplied with pads. High-grade females will have to be taught to attend to their own hygiene and sanitary belts or pants with special inserts for the pads may be used. Instruction in the use of vaginal deodorants can be given. It is not advisable to introduce handicapped female patients to internal sanitary protection, since the insertion of the tampon may be too difficult for them. There is also the risk that they may not be removed with a resulting unpleasant discharge.

The menstrual record of each patient should include notes about the onset of each menstrual cycle, its duration, whether the discharge is normal or excessive, and whether any pain or discomfort is experienced by the patient.

Many handicapped females menstruate infrequently or irregularly, but any missed period in a patient who usually menstruates regularly must be reported.

Other vaginal discharges
Vaginal discharges other than the normal menstrual discharge should be noted and reported. Vulval irritation and subsequent scratching by the patient may be the first evidence of a discharge. The medical staff should be informed and a vaginal swab taken so that a laboratory examination can be made and appropriate treatment prescribed.

Birth control
Methods which depend on the handicapped patient for their correct use

are too unreliable. A coil can be fitted in the uterus but must be checked monthly. Where there is adequate supervision to see that it is taken regularly, 'the pill' can be used, and there is no evidence to show that this encourages promiscuity.

Sterilisation
This may be carried out as the result of medical advice, and with the consent of the next of kin and the patient.

Pregnancy
Whilst mentally handicapped persons can marry and may have children, the mentally handicapped female is not usually capable of looking after a baby adequately. Where both parents are mentally handicapped there is a likelihood that the baby will be mentally handicapped. If the father is known to be of normal intelligence there is a better chance of the baby being normal. Pregnancy is best avoided but, if it occurs, then therapeutic abortion can be considered. This may be unsuitable when the pregnancy is too far advanced, or where there are religious or other objections to termination.

17

Education and Training

In the broadest sense education means the nourishment of the mind, and whilst many who are mentally handicapped may not be educable in the normal scholastic sense, almost all are capable of some development of the mind in response to training. Training must be started as early as possible when the brain is at its stage of greatest development.

The mentally handicapped child tends to be much less active and is less likely to explore and learn in the way normal children do. Because of this it is important for those giving care to take the initiative in stimulating the child and in keeping activities going.

Sensory Training

This is the name given to training which is specifically aimed at developing the senses of touch, hearing, vision, taste and smell, balance, and general coordination and discrimination.

Touch

The development in children of touch and the recognition of objects (including their own body) in relation to other objects depends on handling objects of different shapes and sizes, weight, texture and temperature. Bricks may be built up and knocked down, balls rolled and thrown, shapes of different sizes put into the correct holes and jig-saw puzzles played with. Toys may be soft and cuddly, of bendable plastic, or hard and wooden. Care must be taken to avoid toys with sharp edges, or which are small enough to be swallowed.

Hearing and speech

Hearing is one of the most important senses, as the development of speech and hence communication with others is normally dependent on this.

In addition to talking frequently to the child, rattles, bells and other noises help to gain attention and to develop hearing. People and objects should be pointed at and named to help the development of language. Singing words may sometimes help to do this. Many handicapped people, and especially those with Down's syndrome, have a sense of rhythm and musical games with dancing or hand-clapping are important ways of training in the discrimination of sounds. Percussion bands can sometimes be developed if one or two leaders can be found, and the slower children can follow the leaders.

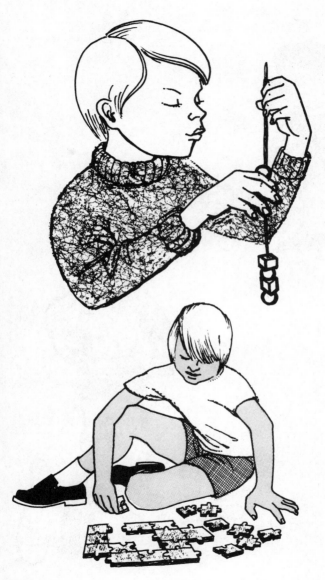

Vision

At birth the two eyes do not focus together and in a normal baby the eyes do not coordinate fully until about six months, and squinting is common until then. If squinting becomes constant then the vision in the weaker eye deteriorates. Vision in both eyes is necessary to develop an appreciation of distance, and of the relative positions of different objects. Many handicapped children are slow in learning to coordinate their eye movements and special treatment may be required to train them in this. Squints which persist may require a surgical operation. The use of different colours is important in training, and contrasting colours can be used in teaching left from right, or in separating children into groups, or in teaching what is permitted or forbidden, as by using green and red signs.

Taste and smell

Taste and smell are developed with different foods. Many children when given a strange object will smell it and put in in their mouths to aid identification.

Balance and coordination

Balance and muscle coordination are often poor in backward and brain-damaged children and because learning is slow great patience and perseverance are required. One of the authors knows a boy with Down's syndrome who did not sit up unaided until aged ten years, and two years later he was walking, and a girl with cerebral palsy following encephalitis who first started to stand (with assistance) when she was aged nineteen years. Balance can be improved by walking along planks raised a few inches from the ground and by using tricycles and scooters. Fine muscle coordination is helped by sorting out beads of different sizes and colours. Other training will involve coordination such as in tying laces and fastening buttons when dressing.

Play Therapy

Play therapy helps in socialisation and gives emotional satisfaction when a group of children join together. Music and movement, ball games, play-acting and reciting nursery rhymes are useful examples. More individual play and expression can be developed with sand trays and drawing or painting. Water play is always popular but needs good supervision and the water must be frequently changed where dirty or incontinent children are concerned.

Training is not only aimed at developing skills, it must also teach self-control so that as a child grows bigger and stronger he does not become a danger to himself or others. In the stage of domestic socialisation (p. 10) training and education depend on approval from those with whom the child has developed a relationship of love and affection. There must be consistency with regard to rewards and punishment. The best reward is praise and the most effective punishment is disapproval, and they must be clearly linked in the child's mind with his behaviour. When the memory is short, praise or punishment should be given immediately so that the child can realise what it is for. Praise and other rewards are sometimes called positive reinforcement when given in relation to a specified pattern of behaviour training. Unwanted behaviour can either be ignored, or positively punished, as by standing in the corner or being put to bed, or being deprived of entertainment. In a group situation such as with children in hospital the behaviour of the group in conforming to the expected pattern is a powerful reinforcer in training. The group also expects the appropriate response by the nurse to any deviant behaviour, for each individual in the group is also in the training situation.

Behaviour Modification and Operant Conditioning

Behaviour modification and operant conditioning are terms applied to a psychological technique which is increasingly used in training programmes for the mentally handicapped. A specific programme of training is designed which deals with one aspect of the person's behaviour, and the progress is carefully monitored. The application of behaviour modification is relevant in toilet training, dressing and undressing routines, in teaching the mentally handicapped to feed themselves, etc. Behaviour modification can also be used to 'unlearn' behaviour patterns which have been acquired and which are inappropriate, or socially unacceptable. It can be used for individuals or applied to groups of mentally handicapped people who have the same learning needs.

The selection of patients who are likely to benefit from a programme, and the design of the programme require the skills of a psychologist and of nurses who have had special training. When the programme has been prepared, other staff, or parents and relatives at home, will be instructed in the day to day running of the programme. It is important that instructions be followed carefully, and that guidance be obtained regularly from the behaviour modification staff, otherwise the learning of the skill may be impaired.

Operant conditioning is more directly under the supervision of a psychologist. In this an undesirable behaviour is studied to see what stimuli produce it and then reinforcing stimuli, which can be either positive or negative, are used in order to change the undesired behaviour.

School

All mentally handicapped children are required to have education. If a child can benefit from, and is fit to go to school, he or she will attend classes. If this is not possible, a teacher will visit the child at home or in the hospital or other institution where he is living. The learning needs, and capabilities of retarded children vary widely, and the teaching plans are designed to meet individual needs and thus develop individual talents. Mentally handicapped children have a short attention span and poor ability to concentrate and this can be improved by regular teaching. Group activities in the classroom and in the playing field are important elements in training for adult life.

A number of children do not mature early enough to derive full benefit from the educational programme before they leave school. For those who are able and willing, adult education classes in reading, writing, dressmaking, swimming, etc. should be available.

Occupational Therapy

This is the name given to treatment designed to occupy the mind and energies of a patient in a way which gives him some satisfaction. The occupation itself stops the patient from feeling useless and if it results in producing a pleasing article for others to admire, a picture for the wall or a mat for the floor, then this gives emotional satisfaction. Occupational therapy usually involves a group of people from different wards and this change of company and environment is in itself therapeutic.

Work Therapy

This is a general term for occupational therapy which is more akin to the kind of work done by ordinary people, from domestic work to helping in the gardens, or with the hospital tradesmen. It is not specifically looked at from a commercial point of view.

Industrial Therapy

This is training under modified factory conditions with the aim of training patients for similar kinds of work and this may enable them to be discharged from hospital. It is usually work of a repetitive nature and has incentives which are financial. Points may be awarded for good production and these are then converted to payment at the end of each week. Much industrial therapy is concerned with doing contract work for local firms, e.g. assembling articles from the separate parts, filling containers, etc. It should be remembered that the main aim is therapeutic and not profit-making and contracts should not become dependent on the therapy staff for their timely completion.

Social Training (Habilitation Training)

Social training is relevant at all stages of a mentally handicapped person's development. Intensive social training in small groups is often practised in hospitals to prepare residents for living in a non-institutional environment such as a half-way house, hostel, or group home.

The successful outcome of intensive social training depends on careful preparation of the handicapped person's programme, based on small group teaching outwith the institutional ward environment, and including conscientious monitoring of progress. This is best achieved where a small group teaching outside the institutional ward environment, and including conscientious monitoring of progress. This is best achieved where a small The aim is to teach all the self-care, communication, housekeeping and social interaction skills necessary for unsupervised living.

The Nurse's Function in Education and Training

Education and training are continuous processes and progress in the mentally handicapped is slow. Success is not only due to periods of intensive training at school or at the training centre. The nurse must be familiar with the aims and objectives set for her patients at school so that she can continue the training process in the ward. She herself also does a great deal of training quite independently of school and training centre.

The nurse is involved in the training of patients in several ways:

1 She sets an example to her patients who copy her habits, mannerisms and speech.
2 She plans and carries out habit training programmes with her patients.
3 She is involved in the process of sensory training.
4 She continues training programmes in the wards which were planned and initiated at school or in the training centre.
5 She initiates and supervises training programmes of patients who are learning domestic skills on the ward.
6 She teaches social skills and good manners.

While it is beyond the scope of this book to give detailed instructions on training methods it is worthwhile listing some of the important points that should be observed by anyone assisting in the training of mentally handicapped patients.

1 Always remember that the patients, especially those who are more able, will copy your manner of speech and some of your habits. Thus you will have to be careful in your choice of words and in the tone of voice you adopt when communicating with your patients. Never do anything in the presence of patients that you do not wish them to copy.
2 Before you attempt to teach your patient any skill, get to know him and gain his confidence. By doing this you will avoid such mistakes as trying too much too soon as this leads to frustration and difficult behaviour.
3 Make the training session short, about fifteen minutes or less. Longer sessions will tire the patient.
4 Get the patient's full attention before you start a training session by providing quiet surroundings which do not distract him, and by starting the session with getting him to do something which you know he can accomplish.
5 Give the patient clear indications of what you want him to do by telling him in a few words, and by indicating to him by gestures what is expected.

6 Praise him verbally immediately he does what is expected of him and reward him at once if the giving of rewards is part of the training scheme.

7 Withhold praise and reward whenever the patient does not cooperate.

8 Take care not to praise or reward any behaviour which is irrelevant to the training programme.

9 Give the patient time to respond; you must work at the pace which suits him.

10 Teach complex skills by breaking them down into small steps, taking one step at a time. Do not proceed to the next step until the preceding one has been mastered.

11 Complex skills, such as dressing, are best taught by starting with the last step that completes the task and working backwards.

12 Be patient and calm and use the same commands and gestures every time until a skill is mastered.

Holidays

Going on holiday gives pleasure to most people and handicapped patients are no exception. Organising an annual change of scenery and participation in stimulating activities not usually available tests the imagination of the nursing staff when they want to ensure that every patient who can enjoy a holiday actually gets one.

Some larger hospitals for the mentally handicapped have a holiday home near the seaside or in the country which they use for their patients. This has the advantage of ready access at all times and can be enjoyed by patients who are quite helpless as it can be adapted to their needs.

Holiday exchanges between hospitals can work well. Small groups of patients accompanied by staff use the facilities of another hospital as a base.

Caravan holidays are enjoyed by patients who are fit enough to cope with the relatively restricted space in the caravan, and a spell under canvas in good weather can give much pleasure to the more active patients.

A holiday with the family can be arranged for a number of handicapped patients whose parents or other relatives are able to have them.

Providing that holidays are organised to meet the needs and capabilities of the individual and that the patient is in the company of staff or relatives whom he knows and trusts, holidays are a welcome change from the usual routine and much appreciated.

The Therapeutic Team

The treatment and care of the mentally handicapped, dealing as it does with their whole life situation, involves people from many disciplines. They have to work together as a team for the benefit of the patient, each contributing from her own specialty as a full member of the team and not being upset when there is some overlap of care which may be given by more than one discipline. In addition to the doctor and nurse the other professionals likely to be involved include the physiotherapist, schoolteacher, speech therapist, clinical and educational psychologist, occupational therapist and social worker.

likely that it will have to be continued in the ward by the nurse during the periods between attendance with the therapists.

In addition to the above there are *voluntary workers* who act as a bridge to the community. They come with their enthusiasm and willingness to help,. Often their most valuable contribution is the time they can give to individual patients in a social and recreational sphere which is outwith that of the professional staff.

Religious adviser

The minister is in a special situation as his concern extends to his own members wherever they are and at all times. All hospitals welcome visits by the patient's own religious adviser and most large hospitals have persons appointed for each of the principal denominations. It is important for the nursing staff to realise how significant the religious adviser's visit may be to certain patients and how his ministerial duties may relieve many of their anxieties. If his appointment is part-time and he has a church 'in the neighbourhood' then his own congregation may be a useful source of voluntary help in the hospital.

It is just as important for the nursing and medical staff to be in good communication with the religious adviser as with all the other members of the therapeutic team.

When a mentally handicapped person is no longer at home it is usually important for the relatives to maintain contact not only with the handicapped person but also with the caring staff. The relatives will be anxious to continue such treatment as they can during periods when the patient is again in their care.

18

Pocket Money and Rewards

The training of the mentally handicapped should include the spending of money and many hospitals have a shop to facilitate this. Patients who are able should have pocket money weekly to spend on small personal items. Those who are not able to shop themselves should not be denied small extras if they can appreciate them, but here the nurse may have to spend the money on behalf of the patients. The amount of pocket money should not be dependent on the patient's ability but may be modified where a patient is unable to use the full amount. It can also be reduced temporariluy in cases of bad behaviour, as a parent would do in disciplining his child.

Monetary rewards may be given for work done irrespective of pocket money. In a hospital where there are patients of very varied ability it is best to base such incentive payments on the attempt to perform an appropriate task rather than on the actual quality of the work done. Whatever system is used it must be simple enough to be understood by the patients or it will not be an incentive, and it must be seen by them to operate fairly, for any apparent unfairness will upset many of the patients.

Savings should be encouraged so that more expensive items, such as a transistor radio, watch or personal clothing can be bought. It is also a help to any patient likely to be discharged to have some money saved up towards this.

Whilst the nurse should not be involved in the book-keeping side of pocket money and rewards, she should be involved in instructing the patients in how to spend their money wisely or to save. As she acts in some respects in place of a parent it is quite proper for her to help with giving out the money to the patients and, if necessary, explaining to some why they are getting less than others. Some patients may have to be discouraged from spending everything at once so that there is nothing left before the end of the week. With young children, or the most severely handicapped, it may be more appropriate for the nurse in charge to make a weekly bulk buy of sweets, etc. which can be given to the patients each day. Adequate safeguards are necessary to protect the nurse from any accusations about missing money. It is desirable that at all stages in the handling of patient's money two members of the staff should be involved, one of them preferably being from the clerical side.

19
The Administration of Medicines

Medicines or drugs are substances which are given to a person for the treatment of disease (physical or psychological) and this includes the relief of symptoms. The two terms—drugs and medicines—are interchangeable since all types of medicines must contain a certain amount of drug or chemical agent.

All medicines should be prescribed, ordered, stored and administered according to the rules and procedures laid out in the parent book of this series (*Modern Practical Nursing Series—Parent Book*. Welsh, Gillespie and Asher). Nurses should always remember that they are responsible for the safe keeping and the safe administration of medicines to their patients and that extra responsibility rests with them when they exercise this function in the care of mentally handicapped persons who may have no appreciation of what they are being given. A similar responsibility will apply to those in charge of hostels, etc. for the mentally handicapped. Some points relating to the care and administration of medicines are specially emphasised since they apply more importantly in hospitals and institutions for mentally handicapped patients.

1 All drugs should be stored in locked cupboards away from patient areas, and special care has to be exercised during the drug administration round so that no patient has access to the medicine trolley.

2 Overstocking of drugs should be avoided, and unwanted stock should be returned to the pharmacy.

3 The keys to the drug storage cupboards and trolley must be carried by the charge nurse, or nurse in charge of the ward, and should be pinned to her person so that they cannot be removed from a pocket.

4 During 'handover', the drug cupboard keys must be *handed* over, from person to person, not laid down on a desk or passed on through a third person.

5 Borrowing of drugs from ward to ward should be kept to a minimum, it should be recorded on a borrowing sheet when drugs are borrowed, and signatures of the nurse and a witness obtained. No patient should ever be employed on running an errand involving the carrying of drugs.

6 In large wards where most of the patients are up and about, extra care must be taken to ensure that no patient is missed, and that nobody is

given his medicine twice. The immediate positive recording of drugs as they are given can help to prevent possible errors. It is also necessary to control the patients during a drug round so that no one can push another patient aside and take his place in the drug round. Two nurses should be involved in the drug round, not only to check the drugs against the prescription, but also to control the patients.

7 Close supervision is needed to make certain that the patients actually take their drugs. Mentally handicapped patients have little insight and many do not appreciate the need to take what is pescribed. Unless each individual patient is closely supervised it is possible for patients not only not to take their drugs but to pass them on to another patient.

8 Patients who vomit or regurgitate food should receive their drugs either well before, or long after meals, as ordered, so that the risk of the drugs being lost with the food is reduced.

9 When a patient is to be given drugs by injection, sufficient staff should be present to ensure the safe administration of the drug should the patient struggle.

10 Patients must be watched closely for any side effects of drugs, especially when some one starts a new drug or when the dose of a drug is increased.

11 If the rules of administration of drugs are intelligently followed, mistakes should not occur. Special vigilance is needed in long-stay patient wards where changes in drugs are less common and could be overlooked. If a nurse feels that an error may have occurred, the only safe way of handling such a situation is to report it immediately to the medical staff and also to the senior nurse on duty.

Whatever method is elected to give a patient drugs the nurse must at all times make sure that the correct patient gets the correct quantity of the correct drug at the correct time via the correct route.

20

Nursing Notes and Records

Nursing Notes

Nursing notes are kept for every patient while he is receiving care in hospital. They may take the form of additional sheets in the patient's medical record, or comprise a separate folder. Many hospitals use a Cardex or similar system of recording.

The first entry is made at the time of the patient's admission and should report fully any observations made on the patient regarding his physical state, abnormalities, behaviour, and abilities, apart from those observations recorded on special sheets, e.g. urinalysis. This information may also be required by the medical staff and may be duplicated if the medical records on a patient are not kept on the ward in the same folder as the nursing notes.

The frequency with which the notes are written up will vary with the patient's response to care. Shortly after admission and during periods of fairly rapid progress, or regression, daily entries may be necessary, whereas at other times weekly entries may suffice. It is good policy to make routine entries, either weekly or monthly, in wards where patients are receiving long-term care and where changes are not obvious.

Once a plan of care has been prepared it should be entered in the notes. Subsequent entries should contain specific references to the patient's behaviour, his progress in relation to his training programme, and any other information that may be relevant. Specific incidents involving the patient should also be entered, irrespective of whether they form the subject of a special report, e.g. accident report, or not.

Routine observations

Observations made routinely at varying intervals are best recorded on special charts so that previous entries may be easily compared with more recent observations.

Observations thus recorded form part of the patient's records and include:

Drug administration records
Weight and height charts
Epileptic seizure charts
Menstrual records
Urinalysis, especially in diabetic patients
Temperature, pulse, respiration charts, etc.

The frequency with which these observations are recorded varies from patient to patient, and as the need arises, but it is important that the information recorded is accurate.

Special observations
Some patients may be the subject of a study by research workers, or undergo special training programmes such as operant conditioning, and then additional observations will have to be made and recorded. In these circumstances the record sheets used will have been specially prepared and the procedure discussed with the persons concerned.

Sometimes the physiotherapist or speech therapist may ask the nursing staff to continue treatment in the ward, and separate record sheets may have to be kept which are then passed on to the department concerned.

Nursing care records serve several purposes:

1 Observations are recorded
2 Progress reports are entered
3 Unusual incidents are reported
4 Treatment given to patients is recorded
5 Teaching of nurses in training.

They are the written record which the nurse uses when:

1 Handing the ward or department over to another nurse
2 Preparing routine day and night reports for the administrative office
3 Preparing special reports
4 Participating in patient assessment conferences.

21
Suggestions and Complaints

Sometimes visitors, patients or staff may wish to make suggestions or complaints and it is important to have simple informal ways in which this can be done so that, where possible, the person making the suggestion or complaint will know that it has been taken note of. Once this has been done most people are prepared to wait and see what action is taken and only if there seems to be no, or insufficient, action taken is the suggestion or complaint taken to a higher authority.

Usually the first step is for the visitor or patient to raise the matter with the charge nurse and, if it cannot be dealt with simply, then it should be put in writing and there should be a book in each ward for suggestions and complaints. The book should have numbered, duplicate pages and the top copy of each entry in the book should go via the Senior Nursing Administrator to the Hospital Secretary or doctor in charge of the patient.

Staff should normally raise matters with their own superiors and joint consultative committees can bring up matters of general import. Many staff are members of a trade union and matters which cannot be dealt with satisfactorily within the hospital may be referred to their union.

Ombudsman or Health Commissioner
This is a commissioner appointed by the Government to investigate complaints of injustice or hardship as a result of failure of a service provided under the National Health Service. The normal channels for dealing with complaints should have been tried first. Certain items are excluded from the jurisdiction of the Ombudsman and these include actions taken solely in the exercise of clinical judgement.

In Scotland the Mental Welfare Commission is an independent official body whose responsibility is the welfare of people with mental disorder. Matters concerning the welfare of any patients in Scotland with mental disorder in hospital or elsewhere can be referred to this body.

22

Legal Provisions

Where Sections are given, e.g. S.60 these are the relevant sections in the
English Mental Health Act, 1959. Sections given in brackets afterwards
are the corresponding sections in the Mental Health (Scotland) Act, 1960,
but for the purposes of court procedure some of these have been
superceded by Sections of the Criminal Procedure (Scotland) Act (1975).
The major change with respect to mental handicap introduced by the
1982 Mental Health Amendment Act is the replacement of the terms
mental subnormality and *severe subnormality* by the terms *mental
impairment* and *severe mental impairment* (page 5) with respect to the
making of a Hospital or Guardianship Order. The 1982 Act also extends
the rights of appeal of those subject to Hospital (Guardianship) Orders
and decreases the interval of time by which they must be reviewed.

Admission to hospital of patients concerned in criminal proceedings
Under Section 60 (Scot. S.55) where a person has been convicted of an
offence and the court is satisfied on the evidence of two medical
practitioners, one being specially approved for this purpose, that the
accused is suffering from mental disorder then the court may authorise
his admission to, and detention in, a specified hospital. Prior
arrangements must have been made for the admission of the offender to
the hospital and the admission must take place within 28 days of the
order.

In a magistrate's court an order for admission to hospital may be made
without having a conviction recorded if the court is satisfied that the
accused committed the offence.

In certain cases, pending a final decision by the court, a person with
mental disorder who has committed an offence may by court order be
admitted to a mental hospital instead of being kept in custody, under
S.68 (Scot. S.54).

A hospital order unless earlier discharged usually lasts for one year
when it must be reviewed by the hospital.

Restriction on discharge
Under S.65 (Scot. S.60) a higher court may order that an offender
detained under a hospital order shall be subject to special restrictions
either without limit of time or for such period as may be specified in the
order. This may be done when it is felt that it is necessary for the

protection of the public. There was formerly no right of appeal against such an order but this is now introduced by the 1982 Act.

Insanity
This term is not used in the Act (but Scot. S.63). The effect of a finding of insanity would be the same as a hospital order restricting discharge without limitation of time.

Compulsory admission to hospital where there are no criminal proceedings
Where a person with mental disorder will not agree to admission to hospital a compulsory order may be obtained under Part IV of the Act. The application is normally made by the nearest relative or a mental welfare officer.

Compulsory admission may be for observation or assessment as well as for treatment but detention for observation shall not exceed 28 days. Compulsory admission for treatment did not extend to persons over 21 years unless there was severe subnormality or mental illness, but the 1982 Act, whilst replacing 'subnormality' by the more restrictive 'mental impairment' also removes the age limit of 21 years. Normally medical certificates are required by two doctors but emergency admission for observation for up to 72 hours can be obtained on one medical recommendation.

Special hospitals
These are institutions for persons subject to detention under the Act who require treatment under conditions of special security on account of their dangerous, violent or criminal propensities.

Effect of a compulsory (or Court) order
This enables the patient to be taken to and kept in the hospital while the order is in force. The Responsible Medical Officer (p. 6) may grant leave of absence as part of the treatment.

Appeals against detention
A Mental Health Review Tribunal is an official body consisting of at least three members, one of whom must be legally qualified and another medically qualified. Appeals on behalf of a patient who is compulsorily detained may be made initially after 6 months (and then annually) to a Mental Health Review Tribunal by the patient, or his nearest relative. After due investigation the tribunal can order the patient's discharge.

In Scotland appeals can be made to the Mental Welfare Commission or to the Sheriff.

Absence without leave (S.40)

A patient who is liable to be detained and who has absented himself from hospital without leave may be taken into custody and returned to hospital within a period of 28 days, unless he is a subnormal patient over the age of 21 years, when the period is 6 months. In Scotland (S.36) the equivalent period for mental defectives is 3 months. Where there is a restriction on discharge prolonged absence does not affect the validity of the order and the patient may be taken into custody at any time.

Ill-treatment of patients

Under the Mental Health Act, 1959, S.126 (Scot. S.95), it is an offence for anyone on the staff of a hospital or mental nursing home to ill-treat or wilfully neglect a patient receiving treatment for mental disorder.

Under S.128 (Scot. S.97) it is an offence for any man on the staff of a hospital or mental nursing home to have unlawful sexual intercourse with a woman who is receiving treatment there for mental disorder.

Under S.127 it is an offence for any man to have unlawful sexual intercourse with a woman who is suffering from severe subnormality unless he does not know and has no reason to suspect her to be severely handicapped. In Scotland (S.96) the offence is extended to any woman who is a defective and also to procuring or encouraging any woman who is a defective to have unlawful sexual intercourse.

Children's hearings

Under the Social Services Act (1970) the institution of Children's Hearings in place of Children's Courts means that now most mentally handicapped offenders under the age of 18 years in hospital are admitted as informal patients, although compulsion can be used if necessary and the courts will still deal with more serious offences.

Probation

This is a form of supervised behaviour open to the Courts where an offence has been committed which does not carry a fixed penalty. Although there is no age limit it is most often used with young people and first offenders. Supervision is carried out by probation officers (social workers in Scotland). The maximum period is 3 years and where the court is satisfied there is mental disorder it may direct that a period (of the probation), not exceeding one year, be spent in a mental hospital.

Patients' correspondence

Under Section 36 (Scot. S.34) of the Act the responsible medical officer may in certain circumstances withhold from the Post Office any postal packet addressed by a *detained* patient but not if it is to a member of parliament, or the managers of the hospital, or any authority or person with power to discharge the patient (e.g. a Mental Health Review Tribunal).

The responsible medical officer may also withhold from a *detained* patient any postal packet addressed to the patient if it would interfere with the patient's treatment or cause him unnecessary distress. The 1982 Act further restricts the circumstances in which postal packets may be withheld.

Northern Ireland

In Northern Ireland there is a Hospitals Authority which is responsible for community as well as hospital care. The term used for the mentally handicapped is 'persons requiring special care' and these are those 'suffering from arrested or incomplete development of mind' which makes them socially inefficient to such an extent as to require supervision, training or control either in their own interests or those of other persons. The appropriate Act dealing with mental disorder is the Mental Health Act (Northern Ireland), 1961.

Legal Aspects Regarding Property

Trustee

When a person is unable, because of his mental state, to understand the extent of his goods and property or is unable to give proper directions for looking after it, then a court may appoint a trustee or curator to act on his behalf. The person appointed is usually a lawyer, accountant or relative. The Court of Protection in England can undertake this duty.

Will

If a mentally handicapped patient wishes to make a valid will then he must be able at the time of making it to have a clear understanding of the nature and extent of his property and also a knowledge of the people who would normally expect to benefit from his will and the relative importance of these expectations. If anyone uses his influence unduly to exert claims on the patient then this would render the will liable to be made invalid.

Contract

A contract or bargain entered into by a mentally handicapped person can be rendered invalid by the person or his representatives if it can be shown that the handicapped person did not understand the nature of the contract and the other party to the contract knew that the person was mentally handicapped.

23
Useful Addresses

National Association for Mental Health,
    39 Queen Anne Street, London W1M 0AJ.
    The Association publishes:
    Mind and Mental Health magazine four times a year.
    Publications list of other Reports, etc. is available on request.
Mencap, 123 Golden Lane, London EC1 Y0RT.
    The Society publishes:
    Parents' Voice—quarterly.
    Directory of Residential Accommodation for the Mentally Handicapped
        in England, Wales and N. Ireland.
    Parents' information bulletins.
The Association of Professions for the Mentally Handicapped,
    126 Albert Street, London NW1 7MF.
British Institute of Mental Handicap,
    Wolverhampton Road, Kidderminster DY10 3PP.

24
Suggested Further Reading

An Outline of Basic Nursing Care — E.M. Welsh, C.A. Asher, M. Gillespie. (Modern Practical Nursing Series, Parent book) William Heinemann Medical Books: London

Psychiatry — E.A. Lee, A.B. Sclare. (Modern Practical Nursing Series) William Heinemann Medical Books: London

Nursing the Mentally Retarded — J. Gibson and T. French. Faber & Faber: London.

Mental Subnormality — W.A. Heaton-Ward. Wright: Bristol.

Care and Training of the Mentally Subnormal — C.H. Hallas, W.I. Fraser and R.C. McGillivray. Wright: Bristol.

The Mentally Handicapped Child — B.H. Kirman. Nelson: Sunbury, Middlesex.

The Educationally Subnormal in the Community — N. Ward. National Elfrida Rathbone Society: London.

The Educable Mentally Retarded Child and his Teacher — S.S. Slaughter. F.A. Davis & Co: Philadelphia.

The Educational Needs of Severely Subnormal Children — M. Stevens. Edward Arnold: London.

Index